C

Pe South
Wh eak Area

Seddon Neudorfer

www.countrysidedogwalks.co.uk

First published in December 2013 by **Wet Nose Publishing Ltd**,
Reprinted January 2016
All enquiries regarding sales telephone: 01824 704398
email cdw@wetnosepublishing.co.uk
www.countrysidedogwalks.co.uk
ISBN 978-0-9573722-6-9

.

 British Library Cataloguing-in-publication data.
A catalogue is available for this book from the British Library. Whilst every effort has been made to ensure that the information in this book is correct, the author or the publisher can accept no responsibility for errors, loss or injury however caused. Maps based upon out of copyright Ordnance Survey mapping.
Printed in Poland by www.lfbookservices.co.uk

Manchester
Dark Peak Area
Stockport
Sheffiel
1
2
3
4
5
6
7
8
9
10
A623
Buxton
Peak District
National Park
11
12
13
14
15
16
A53
White Peak Area
Matlc
17
18
19
20
A515
Leek

Contents

Introduction

The twenty walks included in this book are all designed so that you and your wet nosed friend have a really enjoyable time. Where there are stiles, they are specially designed with lift gates for dogs. At a quick glance there is information at the beginning of each walk to tell you what to expect and what you may need to take with you. The descriptive guides will also warn of any roads ahead or areas of livestock so that you can get your dog on the lead well in advance.

Dogs just love to explore new places. They really enjoy the new smells and carry themselves a little higher with the added excitement. Going to new places gets you and your dog out and about, meeting new people and their dogs. It is important to socialise dogs, as they will be more likely to act in a friendly manner towards other dogs as they gain confidence.

The stunning pictures in this book are just a taster of what you can see along the way. Many of the walks have fantastic views and scenery. Some of the walks are wooded, offering shade on those hot summer days.

The walks are graded Easy, Medium and Challenging. They are all around one to three hours long, depending on your and your dog's pace. You may start with the easy ones and work up to the challenging walks depending on your and your dog's fitness. Different dog breeds and dog age must be taken into account when you decide which walks to do.

Different breeds of dog have different levels of fitness. For example, bulldogs can only do short walks whereas a border collie or a springer spaniel are extremely energetic and difficult to tire out. It is recommended that you do some research on the breed of dog that you own to get to know what sort of exercise that they require.

You may have a walk that you are happy doing with your dog every day, but this book will show you new areas to explore with a change of scenery and a chance to meet new people and their dogs. Dogs love new places to visit and you will see the change in them as they explore the new surroundings, taking in the new smells with delight. You will fulfil both your life and your dog's just by trying somewhere new.

Some of the walks include bridleways, so you may encounter horses and cyclists. It is important to put your dog on a lead if you see horses approach. It is always helpful to say hello to the riders as they near so that the horse realises that you are not a threat.

The Peak District National Park

In 1951 the Peak District was the first area in the UK to be designated as a National Park. It lies in central and northern England, mainly in Derbyshire but covering small areas of Staffordshire, South and West Yorkshire, Cheshire and Greater Manchester.

The majority of land within the National Park is privately owned, consisting mostly of agricultural land. The National Trust own 12%, and the National Park Authority own 5%, several water companies are also major land owners, however the National Park Authority oversees land management throughout the park and planning restrictions protect the area from inappropriate development and land use.

The north (Dark Peak) and south (White Peak) differ greatly. The north is dominated by vast open moorland, with several reservoirs and forest plantations. The exposed bedrock is mostly gritstone which is dark in colour, which can be seen throughout, with many cliff faces, rock stacks and rock formations. The south has many dales and steep sided natural woodland, with rivers flowing through the bottom. The bedrock is mostly limestone, which is white in colour and is also highly visible with many cliff faces rising up from the valley floor.

Visitors to the National Park would be forgiven in thinking that they are miles from any town or city, but in fact the cities of Manchester and Sheffield lie on the boundaries, sandwiching the National Park in the middle.

Ground Nesting Birds

Watch out for vulnerable ground nesting birds during 1st of March until the end of July. Dogs that stray off the main paths may disturb birds and chicks, possibly killing them or breaking eggs. Species to look out for are Sky larks, Meadow pipits, Curlew, Red and Black grouse, Snipe and Pheasants.

Some if not all of these birds are declining in numbers, due partly to their vulnerability when nesting. Dogs are a threat to them, even if treading on them unintentionally. Some other threats are foxes, badgers, stoats, weasels, birds of prey and crows.

Please help to protect these birds during the nesting season by keeping your dog on the paths when walking in open areas such as grassland, moors, heathland and scrub.

Rivers

Some dogs love water and will think nothing of plunging into the river. With the extreme weather conditions over the last few years, a river that may be safe for your dog to swim in can change in a matter of hours to become a swollen torrent that could wash your dog away. Please be careful when near rivers if there have been heavy periods of rain or if they look swollen or fast flowing. It is best to put your dogs on the lead, until you have assessed the situation.

Livestock

If you find that you need to cross a field with cattle or horses and they seem interested in you or your dog it is recommended within the Countryside Code to let your dog off the lead. Never try to get between livestock and your dog. Your dog will get out of a situation a lot more easily with speed than you can. It is usually only cattle with young calves that are a threat, or young heifers or bullocks that tend to get a little inquisitive. They will usually stop when they get close to you or your dog.

Most horses will come over for a fuss but a small proportion do have a problem with dogs. They may see them as a threat and will act to defend the herd. Horses that are out with a rider are completely different as they are not defending the herd, and as long as you keep a safe distance there should not be a problem.

Sheep are not a danger to you, but your dog can be a danger to them. Where sheep are grazing it is vital that you have your dog on a lead or under very close control. You will know your dog, but if you are unsure it is better to play safe and keep your dog on a lead. It is important always to have your dog on a lead when around lambs. Lambs have a higher pitched bleat and can be the size of a cat, and your dog may act differently amongst them.

Ticks

If you have been walking in areas where sheep graze you should check your dog for ticks. They must be removed as soon as possible. It is best to use tick tweezers, which are specially designed to remove the head and leg parts of the tick. Ticks can carry diseases and the longer they remain latched on to your dog the more the chance of spreading infections.

Forests

The forest walks in this book are a changing landscape, which makes them unique and interesting. Descriptions may change with time, for instance a path may be described as being in the shade of the forest, but as this is a worked forest a section could be clear felled at any time. Another change over the years could be where a view is described across a previously felled area. This could then be planted up and trees grown blocking the views. Paths may change but this is less likely. On rare occasions the Forestry Commission may temporarily close paths due to forest works but again this is even less likely on a weekend. Any changes to the path networks that may occur after the date of print will be updated on our website.

Does your dog fetch a stick?

Most dogs love sticks and will pick them up without any encouragement from their owners. Vets and dog trainers recommend that you should not throw sticks for dogs. They can cause nasty injuries, sometimes fatal as the stick can pierce the throat, or rebound off the ground and cause harm to your dog.

Please clean up after your dog

Always be prepared, having dog bags with you at all times. Once you have cleaned up after your dog, please keep the bag, until you see a bin. If there are no bins provided, then take it away with you to a roadside bin. Dog bags that are discarded on the paths or in the bushes are unpleasant and unsightly and will not degrade.

1. Padley Gorge

Medium - 2.7 miles - 1hr 30min

This is a wonderful circular walk, starting in the Longshaw Estate. You will travel into wider estate grounds, following beside the Burbage Brook, into the most stunning woodland. The deeper into the gorge you travel the more atmospheric it gets, with the wonderful ancient woodland spreading across both sides of the river. Many ferns and boulders covered in moss spread across the woodland floor, and busy wood ants cross your path in summer. This truly is a magical place and a must for you and your dog. There are sheep and a quiet breed of cattle in some parts of the walk. There are no roads, except one to cross. Dogs must be kept on a lead whilst in the Estate grounds.

How to get there – From Hathersage continue on the A6187 in the direction of Sheffield. Turn right following the signs for the National Trust Longshaw Estate. Turn right following the sign for the car park and Longshaw Estate visitor centre.

Grid Reference – SK 266800 **Nearest Postcode –** S11 7TS

Parking – National Trust Woodcroft Car Park pay and display

Facilities – There is a shop/café visitor centre and toilets

You will need – Dog lead, dog bags and sturdy footwear

The Walk

❶ Keep your dog on a lead while in the estate gardens at the beginning of the walk. From the car park, pass the pay and display and an interpretation panel on your left, following the well-made path. Go over a bridge, passing between the stone walls.

On reaching a path, turn right, ignore a left turn and continue until you reach another path.
❷ Turn left and a little further along take the path on the right, passing the visitor centre and benches to the left, walking alongside the stock fence on your right, with farmland on the other side.

Pass through a gate and enter into the shade of several yew trees. Stock may be grazing on this section of the walk. There may be sheep or cattle, but the cattle are a quiet breed and used to people. Continue straight ahead on a path lined with yew, beech and rhododendrons. The trees and rhododendrons on the left clear, where you will have views across farmland to the hills beyond.

Pass through another gate, where the area opens up into stock fields, with sheep or cattle. You will see a lake on your far right. On reaching rhododendrons once again, pass through a gate into deciduous woodland.

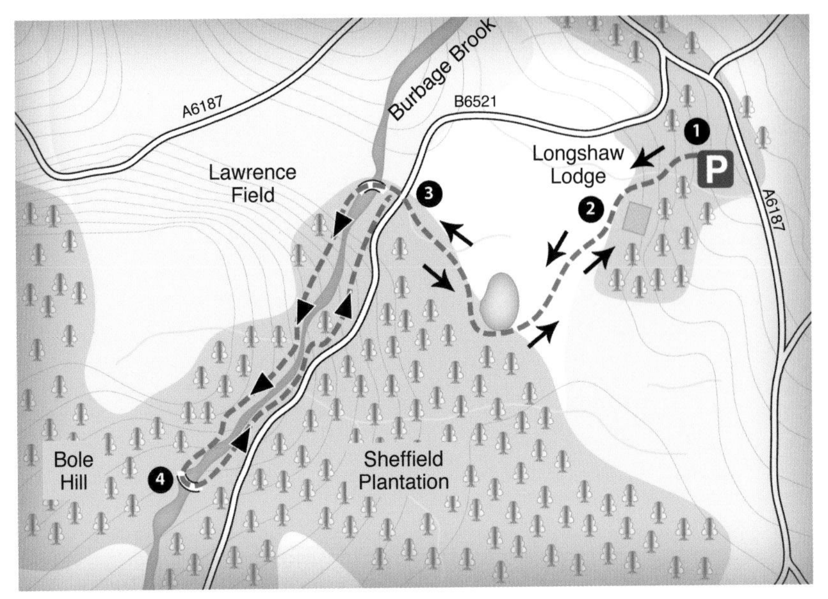

After passing through another gate you will reach the lake and mature well-spaced pine and beech trees, with rhododendrons.

Follow on the path beside the lake, continuing through beech woodland and then passing a stone outbuilding on your right. Then pass through another gate. Ignore a path on your left and continue on the gravel path. You will reach another stone building, 'The Discovery Barn', with interpretation panels inside. Pass the building and continue to the road. Keep your dog on a short lead and go through the gate to cross the road. ❸

Pass through a gate on the opposite side and descend the steps. Ignore a path on the left and continue straight ahead towards the river. This is a wonderful open area, with pockets of heather, boulders and trees that line the river. Cross the footbridge, where your dog can have a soak in the water. Turn left and follow the river, passing boulders and a little further along you will pass another foot bridge, with lovely split timber rails.

The boulders become larger and plentiful as you continue along the path. You enter into lovely gnarly oak woodland. Go through a gate and continue, now descending on a rocky path with exposed bedrock. The path veers away from the river for a while, with ferns and bilberry spreading across the woodland floor.

As you become parallel to the river once again, it is far below you. Cross over a crystal-clear stream as it makes its way to the river. Ignore a path on your

right signed for Surprise View and continue. A little further along you will reach a fork in the path. Take the right path, where just after on the left you will see a discarded carved millstone.

A little further along look out for a way-marker on your left, just before the path ascends with stone steps. Turn a sharp left here to descend deeper into the gorge. Descend the steps to reach another path and turn right. Pass a stone bench and descend more stone steps then cross a bridge over the river, stopping half way across to watch the river from both sides. In the heart of the gorge, this is truly a breath-taking experience: the atmosphere absorbs into your soul. Stop here a while and enjoy.

❹ After crossing the bridge turn right and proceed to the steps. Once you are at the top turn left on the worn path. Ignore a path that descends back down to the river and continue on a gradual ascent. There are steps on the steeper sections. There is a road on your far right, so keep dogs under close control. Again the river is now below you on your left.

Ignore another path on your left that descends to the river. Continue ascending straight ahead, calling your dog close as the path follows close to the road, passing an exit onto the road. Continue straight ahead, now ascending over a rocky section. Just afterwards there is another rocky section with a descent, crossing a stream and then ascending back onto the path.

The path now follows a high stone wall on your right, with the river below on your left. You will reach another stone wall; pass between the two stone walls and then take the path on your right. Leaving the old stone wall, follow the well-worn path.

You will pass a path on your left, staying on the wider path to the right. On reaching a fork, stay on the higher path, parallel with the road. Cross over exposed stone, passing another old millstone to your right, just as you come close to the river once again on your left.

Continue on the path, between the river and the road, passing over rocks and heading towards the stone wall. Pass through a gate at the end of the stone wall and continue following the river below. You will pass some old stone posts and then the lovely familiar footbridge on your left.

Continue on the path which will veer right towards the road, crossing the road once again, and continue through the estate grounds to retrace your steps. Remember to turn left after passing the lake. After passing Longshaw Lodge and the visitor centre turn right and then turn left back to the car park.

2. Froggatt

Challenging - 3.5 miles - 2hrs 30min

This is a wonderful circular walk through stunning deciduous woodlands, with moss-covered boulders scattered on the woodland floor. You will pass through the lovely, quiet village of Froggatt, and then through wonderful woodland, climbing and meandering until you reach the top of a cliff face, know as Froggatt Edge. Beautiful scenery and fantastic rock formations and stacks make the climb worth the effort. There are streams throughout the walk. Sheep and cattle may be present and there are quiet lanes.

How to get there - Take the A6187 from Sheffield, heading towards Hathersage. Turn left onto the A625 signed for Froggatt. Shortly after passing the Grouse Inn on your right hand side, take a right turn, following the brown National Trust sign for parking.

Grid Reference – SK 255777
Nearest Postcode – S11 7TZ

Parking – Pay and display National Trust Haywood car park

Facilities – There are no facilities

You will need – Dog lead, dog bags

The Walk

1 From the car park start with your back to the pay and display, where you will see a finger-post on the opposite side and to your left. Take the path straight ahead, following the sign for Nether Padley.

Cross over a path and continue straight ahead, descending towards the post and rail fence. Pass through the gate into the mixed deciduous woods, with a rock face on your right. The path is slightly rocky in places and will level off, cutting across the hillside.

2 On reaching a fork, take the left path, which descends. There are many moss-covered boulders and bracken dominates the woodland floor. On meeting another path, which crosses the path that you are on, turn left.

You will pass a small crypt-like waterworks building on your right and then cross a stream, where your dog can get a drink. Continue on the path, which widens out a little. On reaching a stone wall, pass through the gate, putting your dog on a lead or under close control.

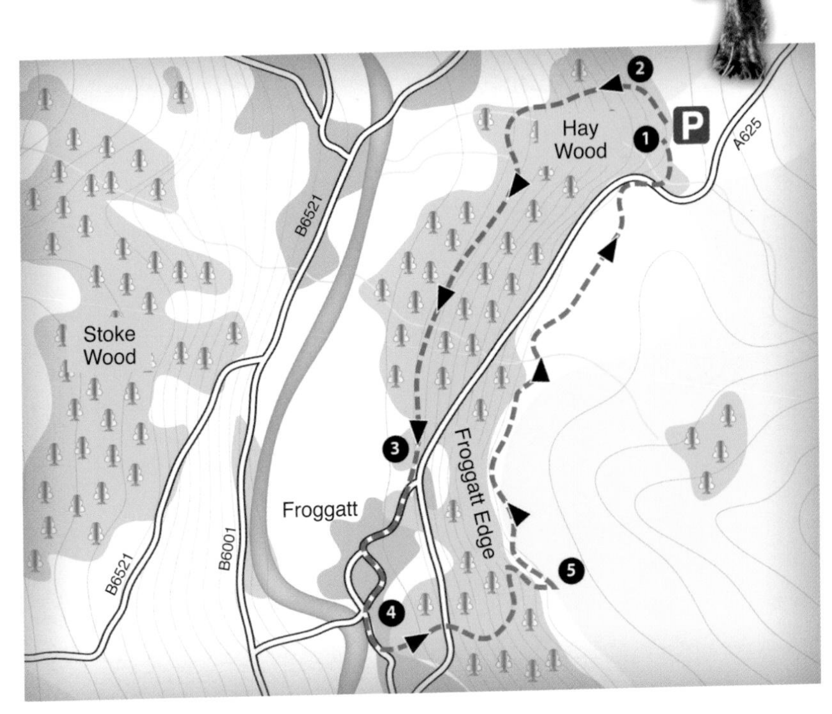

Pass through the hillside pasture, with lovely views on your right of beautiful countryside and the village of Grindleford. Ignore a path which veers to your left, and continue straight ahead, passing through a gate back into woodland.

Follow the worn path, crossing another stream. Pass remnants of a stone wall, then crossing another stream and continue straight ahead. You will reach a stone wall, where you pass through the gap. The path will get a little boggy for a short section as you descend.

Ignore a path on your right and continue. The path may get a little overgrown and narrow for a short section. On meeting another path, turn left and cross a stream using the stepping stones. The path widens out again here. Pass an old stone post on your right, where bilberry is abundant on the woodland floor.

Cross another stream, then ignore a path on your right, and continue, now ascending. You will pass a large rock boulder on your left and a stream will cross under the path. Continue on a long, gradual ascent.

You will walk alongside an ancient stone wall on your right, and then pass between old stone gate posts, where you will then walk between two stone walls. Put your dog on a lead, as there is a road ahead. At the end of the path, pass through the gate onto a quiet road, turning right. ❸

Descend through Froggatt Village, passing Frog Hall on your right. Ignore a footpath on your left and continue, turning left onto Malthouse Lane. Pass a road on your left and continue, rounding a bend to your right, now on The Green. At the end of The Green, turn left onto Hollow Gate. ❹ Pass a road bridge on your right and continue onto Froggatt Lane. Just as the road ascends, before the bend, turn left onto the footpath, passing through the squeeze posts; then go through the kissing gate and ascend the glade, keeping your dog on a lead, as there is a busy road ahead.

Pass through a small block of woodland and then back into the meadow, which in the summer months is full of black knapweed and ragwort, a haven for bees and butterflies. Pass through a gate at the end of the meadow and cross the busy road with care.

Take the footpath on the opposite side of the road, into mixed deciduous woodland. The path ascends, a little steeply in places. Keep your dog on a lead until you are well away from the road.

Cross over some exposed bedrock along the well-worn path. There are large boulders that are green with moss and bracken dominates the woodland floor. You will meet a stone wall further along. Pass through the gate, now keeping your dog under close control or on a lead, as there may be sheep or cattle here.

Continue ascending through the wonderful woodland. The path gets a little rocky in places. As you climb, you will see a large rock face ahead and to your right. This is where you are headed.

On meeting another path, turn right, walking with the rock face on your left. A more gradual ascent brings you out onto the top of the rock face, known as Froggatt Edge. ❺ On reaching another path, turn left and follow the well-worn path, out into the open. Sheep and cattle may be grazing, so ensure you have your dog under close control or on a lead. Ground-nesting birds may also be present from March until the end of July.

Follow the neat stone wall on your right, with fabulous views on your left. Take care here; there are dense bracken stands. If your dog chases game birds or rabbits he may not see the cliff face. It may be best to keep him on a lead.

The shapes of the boulders and rock stacks are amazing. You will reach some scattered silver birch that will become woodland as you continue. As you pass a farm gate, take the small gate on your left. Your dog will find water here from the stream on your left.

Continue on this level path through the silver birch woodland for some distance. When you pass a large rock boulder on your left put your dog on a lead, as there is a busy road ahead. The path descends, with a stone wall on your left. Pass through the gate and continue straight ahead, crossing the road just before the footpath ends.

Descend the steps, then follow the rocky path, crossing a stream. Pass through a gap on reaching a stone wall and then ascend on the well made path. When you meet a fork take the right-hand path into oak woods, where you will reach the car park.

3. Curbar Edge

Medium - 2.8 miles - 1hr 30min

This is a fantastic circular walk with stunning panoramic views across miles of beautiful countryside. You will be following along the cliff faces for much of the walk. The rock formations are fantastic and very typical of the Peak District. You will then descend into amazing natural oak and silver birch woodland with moss-covered rock boulders, scattered amongst the woodland floor. There may be cattle and sheep grazing and ground-nesting birds during the nesting season. The walk finishes with a quiet road.

How to get there – From Bakewell take the A619 signed for Chesterfield. At the roundabout follow the sign for Manchester and Stockport on the A623. At the mini roundabout, turn left and continue through the village. Continue on this road, turning right when you see signs for Froggatt and Curbar. After passing the church turn right onto Curbar Hill. The car park will be found on your left beyond the village, and after passing the lay-bys on the side of the road.

Grid Reference – SK262747

Parking – Pay and Display

Facilities – There are no facilities

You will need – Dog leads, water for your dog

The Walk

❶ From the car park, standing with your back to the entrance of the car park, go to the left hand side, where you will find a pedestrian exit leading to a path beside a stone wall. Turn left on the path and follow beside the stone wall on your right. Keep your dog under close control or on a lead, as there may be livestock grazing. A little further along, after passing a picnic bench on your left pass through a kissing gate into an open area. Follow the well-made path, with farmland on your right and heather on your left.

After a short distance, you will see exposed rock faces, and amazing, panoramic views, over miles of countryside. Follow the cliff edges for some way and as you continue, the views open up ahead and to your left.

❷ A little further along cross some large stone slab pavers over a boggy area, where dogs can cool off. The farmland is far off to your right now, with heathland on both sides, giving a real feel of open space, with constant views in all directions. The rock formations are tremendous and typical of the Peak District.

Some distance on, ignore a grassy path on reaching a fork, and keep to the left on the well-made path. Descend a small section of rock and descend on the path.

Where the bracken dominates there may be rabbits or game birds. If your dog is likely to give chase, it may be better to keep him on a lead, as your

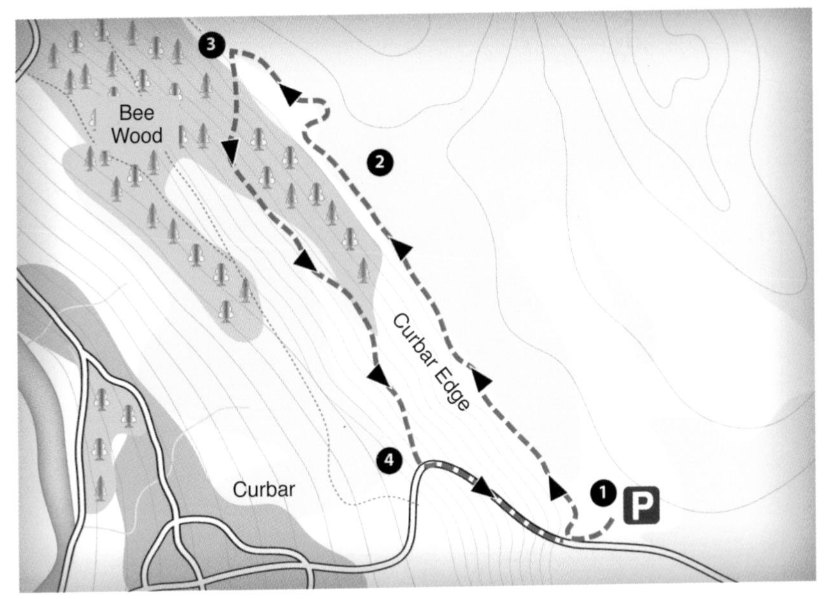

dog could go over the edge: the drop will be unseen because of the long bracken.

As you reach silver birch trees on your left, look for a path on the left just beyond the first clump of trees, which is indicated by a way-marker.

Take this path, passing between bracken, which in summer can encroach the path. The path turns left, just before reaching a rock face. ❸ The path immediately descends quite steeply, and is rocky, so care should be taken if the bracken is high as it will be difficult to see the rocks.

The path will then reach a steep-sided, wooded slope. Pass beside huge rock boulders, into the oak and silver birch woodland. There are many moss-covered rock boulders strewn across the woodland floor, with bracken understory.

The path levels off and cuts across the hillside, and you will eventually reach a stone wall which runs beside you on your right for a short distance. The path then veers away to the left. On entering into woodland clearings you will have views on both sides: to your right of the countryside beyond and to your left of the cliff faces.

After an ascent the path levels off and you will pass a large stone on your left, which is popular for bouldering. You will then pass a house on your right, below. Descend to the gate, putting your dog on a lead before going through it. Continue on the path to the road. ❹ Turn left and ascend the quiet road, where you will have views to your right. You will eventually reach the car park.

4. Chatsworth

Medium - 4 miles - 2hrs

A wonderful circular walk in the grounds of the Chatsworth Estate, packed with charm. You will walk along the River Derwent, with a beautiful weir, amongst pasture land, and then pass the glorious Chatsworth House and shortly after, you will enter into the charming village, Edensor. Then there is an ascent over rolling hilly pasture land, through some woodland and passing under fantastic mature parkland trees. Dogs will have to be on a lead whilst on this walk as there may be cattle, deer and sheep.

How to get there – From Bakewell, take the A6 heading for Matlock. On reaching the village of Rowsley, turn left onto the B6012 following the brown signs for Chatsworth. Continue on this road then turn left, following signs for the garden centre and Calton Lees car park.

Grid Reference – SK 258684
Nearest Postcode – DE4 2NX

Parking – Calton Lees Pay and Display

Facilities – There is a tea room on reaching Edensor Village with outside seating.

You will need – Dog lead, dog bags

The Walk

❶ From the car park go onto the road and head towards the entrance to the garden centre, turning left on a path just before the entrance. Descend into the woodland, turning left just before the end of the path.

On reaching the road, turn right, cross over and take the footpath on the other side just before going over the road bridge. ❷ Follow the river up-stream on your right. You are now walking amongst the estate grounds, where deer roam and sheep and cattle graze. There are mature parkland trees scattered across the pasture, offering shade on hot days if you want to picnic beside the river.

Pass a lovely ruined building to your left and you will see a beautiful weir ahead. Continue on the path, where you will see the weir up close as you pass, where the water tumbles over the rocks. As the worn path ends, continue alongside the river.

The path veers away from the river as you meet larch trees and a post-and-rail fence on your right. Then, as you pass amongst mature beech trees, you will see Chatsworth House to your far right. You will soon be opposite the impressive, grand house, across the other side of the river. Head to the majestic bridge, with its fine statues. Don't cross the bridge, but cross the road and turn left. ❸

Follow the path, which veers away from the road, and ascends a little towards the trees. You will then descend towards Edensor Village. On reaching the road, cross over and go through the small, unusual gate to avoid the cattle grid.

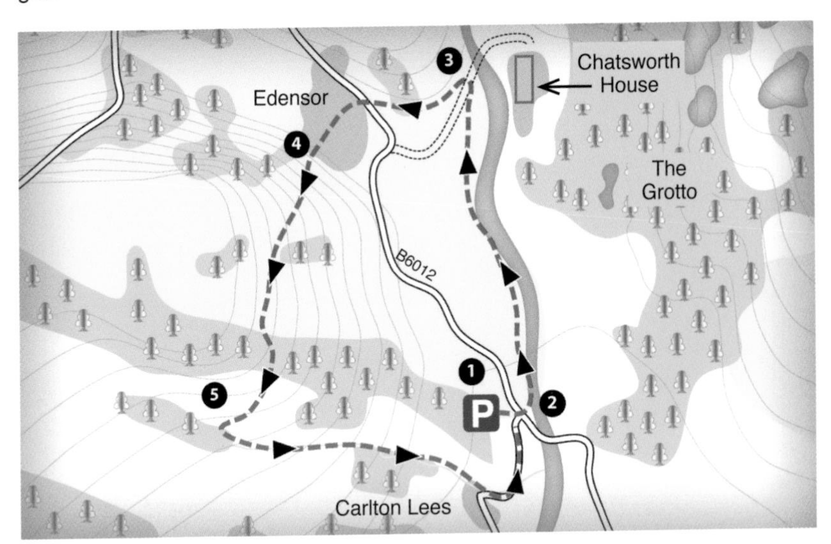

Take the road on the left, which will take you toward a tea-room, and then turn right just before reaching the tea-room, passing the church on your left. Pass some cottages and then after passing Shepherds Cottage, take a footpath on your left signed Calton Lees and Rowsley. Ascend the steps, turning left part-way up. Then pass through a gate and a squeeze-gap in the iron fence. ❹

Cross the open pasture, diagonally to the right. You will pass a way-marker: follow the direction of the arrow, heading toward a bench beneath an oak tree. There are many mature parkland trees throughout. Make your way toward a gap between two blocks of trees, ahead and in the distance, which are fenced off from grazing. Pass the tree enclosure on your left, following the worn path, ascending the hill straight ahead.

Continue to ascend the steep hill, towards the trees ahead. Pass beneath the mature beech trees, where you will see another tree enclosure on your left and a way-marker ahead. On reaching the way-marker take the path straight ahead, continuing with an ascent, and on reaching the woodland and boundary fence, turn left to pass through a gate into the woodland. Continue between the stone wall and the stock fence, passing through a gate at the end of the woods.

Continue straight ahead, following the well-worn grassy path across the middle of a field. Cross another path and continue straight ahead, where you reach a stone wall at the edge of the field. Continue on the path, with the stone wall on your left. ❺ When you reach a gate on your left, pass through it. You will now descend between the stone walls, passing between houses.

The path then snakes around the steep sided hill. Continue to follow the access road, now with a stone wall on your right. There is beautiful countryside scenery ahead of you. Pass through a gateway, staying on the access track as you enter into another field. You will pass some impressive mature oak trees along the track.

You pass a fantastic, ancient alder tree on your left and a stream follows the path on your right, where your dog can cool off. Mature trees offer some shade on hot days. A little further along the track you will pass a lovely old water trough on your left, which still provides water. Continue on the track, with woods now on your right.

Stay on this path for quite a distance, passing mature trees and hawthorns. The track will meet a quiet road, continue straight ahead, ignoring the footpath on your right. You will reach the car park on your left a little further along the road.

5. Bakewell

Medium - 4.7 miles - 2hrs 30min

This is a lovely circular walk, starting in the heart of Bakewell. A walk along a quiet lane will bring you to the beginning of the long distance path The Monsal Trail. This is a disused railway, still with train stations. The path is also popular with cyclists. On leaving the path you will follow a bridleway through some stunning countryside with fabulous views over Bakewell and the surrounding area, walking between two stone walls which keep the cattle at bay. On returning into Bakewell, you will cross a couple of fields which may have cattle grazing, but they are well used to people and dogs and there is an alternative route if you prefer. Your dog will find lots of water along the way.

How to get there – The car park can be found off Bridge Street in the centre of Bakewell, close to the road bridge on Coombs Road.

Grid Reference – SK 220686

Parking – Long stay - Pay and Display

Facilities – There are no facilities

You will need – Dog leads, dog bags

The Walk

❶ Go out of the entrance to the car park and turn left onto the access road. At the end of the access road, turn right. Continue along this road for a good distance (¾mile), passing houses at first and then amongst farmland, between hedgerows.

❷ Just before the viaduct take the footpath on the left, signed for Monsal Trail. This is the beginning of a long distance path on an old disused railway line. Ascend steeply up the path to begin with. Follow the well-made path between the trees, where you will have wonderful views of the hilly countryside. A little further along you will see across to Bakewell.

There is sloped grassland on your right, with grazing sheep. Ensure that your dog doesn't go through the fencing, as it is only post and rail and small dogs may get through to chase the sheep. There are farm fields and horse paddocks on your left. Again, a little further along the fencing on the left is plain wire strands and small dogs may get through. There is deciduous woodland on both sides of the path, with dappled sunlight on warm days.

A little further along you will reach a small stream running on the right hand side where your dog can get a drink. Wild flowers line the path on both sides. You will pass under an arched bridge, where again there is flowing water for your dog to cool off. Ignore a footpath on your right and continue straight on, where you will pass under another arched bridge. Call your dog close

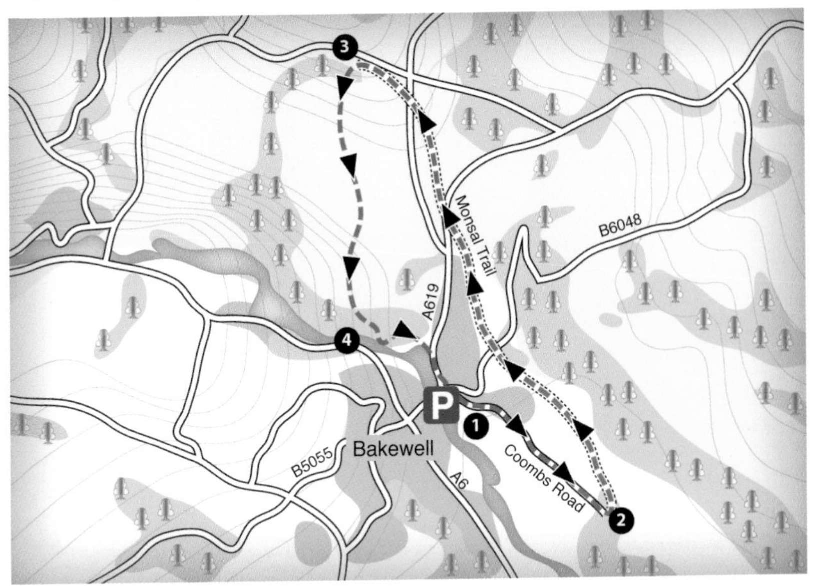

because there is a car park beyond the bridge. You will pass the old Bakewell railway station and car park on your left.

Keep your dogs close for the next section, as there are roads below the slopes and the fence type is unknown. You will pass some houses on your left and then go under another arched bridge, keeping your dog under close control as there is a busy road crossing the bridge.

You will now leave the roads behind, as you continue between farmland. There are now embankments rising up on both sides of the path. A little further along the area will widen out, with picnic benches. Then keep to the left to pass another car park and the old Hassop station. This is now a popular café and gift shop, where you can choose to take a well-earned rest.

Continue on the path and look out for the bridleway on your left, a little further along. ❸ Go through the gate onto the bridleway, ascending to begin with between the stone wall and the woodlands. After passing the woods on your right, you will then be walking between two stone walls, with farmland on both sides.

Pass through a number of gates, where as you climb you will have wonderful views of the hills and countryside, with Bakewell and the church spire. There are wild flowers growing in places on both sides of the path. Put your dog on a lead or under close control when you reach the end of the stone walls. There are sheep grazing on the other side. Pass through a gate, pass a circular mill pond on your right and continue on the grassy path walking through the middle of the field. There are parkland trees and some woodland copse.

Head for the church spire and soon you will pick up a stoned track. On reaching woodland, pass through a gate. Descend on the track, passing some disused sheds on your left. At the end of the track pass a lovely building, Holme Hall, and turn right, passing beside buildings. On reaching the road, turn left opposite a fantastically designed bridge. ❹ Cross the road and follow a stone wall beside a field.

(There may be cattle for the last section of the walk. If you don't wish to walk amongst them, you can follow beside the field on the pavement and continue beside the road. Follow the field around, turning right at the end of the road. Continue with the field on your right and a little further along you will reach a road bridge and the car park on your right).

Take the footpath on your left crossing the stone wall. When you pass through the gate, keep your dog on a lead or under close control and follow the well-worn path crossing the field, towards the river. You will reach two gates. Take the right-hand gate and pass alongside the river. Pass through another gate and follow the gravel path, passing a number of benches beside the river. Take either path ahead and go through the gate onto the road. Cross the road and enter the car park.

6. Monsal Dale

Easy - 2.6 miles -1.5hr

This is a beautiful linear walk following the lovely River Wye, with an amazing weir, amongst some lovely woodlands and meadows that are full of flowers in the summer months. There may be cattle grazing, but they are a quiet-natured breed, and used to dogs and people walking this popular route. There is a busy road to cross at the beginning of the walk.

How to get there – Take the A6 from Bakewell, heading towards Buxton. Pass a road on your left signed for Sheldon. The car park will be on the left hand side about a mile further along the road.

Grid Reference – SK 170705

Parking – White Lodge car park. Pay and display

Facilities – There are toilets in the car park

You will need – Dog lead, dog bags

The Walk

❶ Put your dog on a lead to begin this walk. From the car park pass the pay and display on your left and take the pedestrian exit on your right, where you will reach a set of steps onto the busy road. Take this path, crossing the road with care. Pass through a squeeze-gap in the stone wall, descend the steps and follow the well-made path across the hay meadow.

Cross the stile, where dogs can pass through the gap provided. Larger breeds of dog can go to the left where the gap is greater. There are a small number of cattle throughout the walk so dogs must be kept under close control. Cross a stream, where your dog can get a cool drink. Take the path straight ahead, signed Monsal Head.

Continue along the well-worn path with a barbed wire fence on your right, passing through the ash-dominated woodland, with hazel and hawthorn understory. Cross another stream, then the path will lead to a river on your right. Continue up-stream of the river where the area opens out into a meadow.

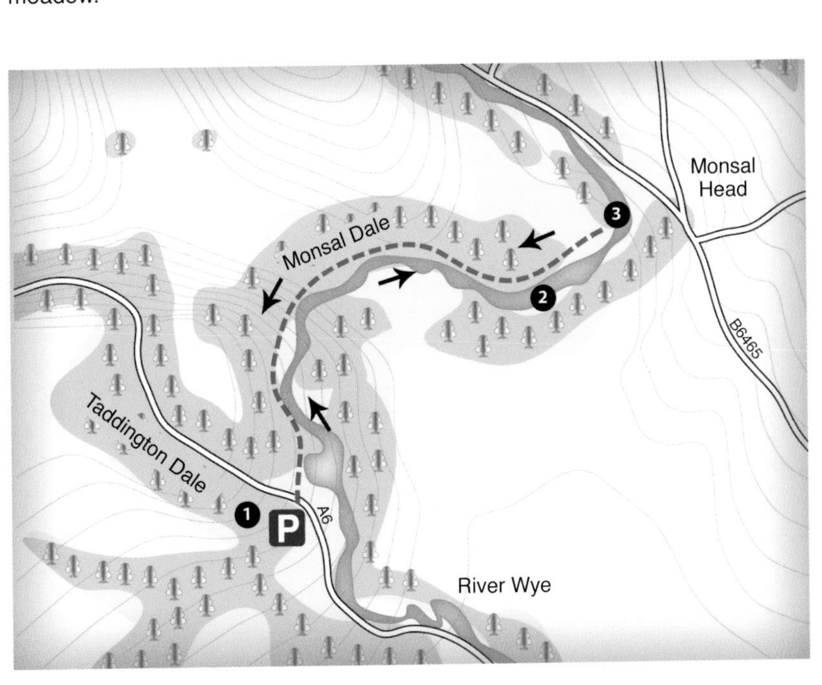

The river is on your far right. Follow the well-worn path through the meadow, surrounded by trees. Continue back into the woods, ignoring any minor paths and you will soon be beside the river once again.

You will pass through another, larger meadow. Ignore a bridge on your right and just afterwards you will see a stunning weir. ❷ This is a lovely place to stop for a while if the cattle are not in the area. There may be grey wagtail and dippers bobbing about along the river.

Continue on, where you will come very close to the weir. You will pass through a gate a little further along. The area will open up again into a small meadow, with the almost still, dammed section of the river here. Continue on the well worn path, where you will see the magnificent Headstone Viaduct ahead. Your dog will enjoy the river here, splashing in and out on hot days. On reaching the end of the meadow, you are at the furthest point of your walk. ❸ Simply turn around and retrace your steps back to the car. Remember to put your dog on a lead before reaching the stile to ensure he doesn't cross the busy road.

7. Monk's Dale

Medium - 3.6 miles - 2hrs

This is a fantastic circular walk, but for large breeds of dog there is the option to make it a linear one because of the narrow squeeze-gaps. The first section of the walk travels through the wonderful Monk's Dale, following a river bed, which dries up during low rainfall. The woodland is absolutely fantastic, dominated by oak. Deep in the valley there is a real ancient feel and a fantastic atmosphere; you will be following a well-trodden path (which can get a little rocky, and slippery after rainfall). Half way around, there is a squeeze-gap in the wall, then an ascent on a quiet road. You will then pass through farmland between stone walls following a bridleway. There may be sheep/ cattle for some short sections of the walk.

How to get there – From Buxton follow the A6 towards Bakewell but take the B6049 following for Tideswell. Miller's Dale car park will be signed after passing through Miller's Dale village on the right hand side of the road.

Grid Reference – SK 138732 **Nearest Post Code** – SK17 8SN

Parking – Pay and Display

Facilities – There are toilets in the car park and a mobile snack bar

You will need – Leads, dog bags and sensible footwear

The Walk

❶ From the car park go back onto the road and turn left, ascending the hill. At the sharp left bend in the road, take the footpath on the right over the stone stile and walk between the fence and the stone wall. ❷ There is farmland on the right. Pass through a kissing gate and keep your dog under close control or on a lead, as there may be livestock. Turn left on the worn path, following beside the stone wall on the left.

Soon you will be amongst the trees heading into the valley. There is exposed rock in places. The path will descend, cross a footbridge and continue to follow the worn path. You will see rock faces to your right and also on the left through the trees. The woodland is stunning, dominated by ash with a section of hawthorn. There are lovely glades and woodland pasture.

On reaching a fork keep to the left, following close to a stream. Soon you will reach a stone wall on the left. Follow beside the stone wall, passing rocky outcrops on your right. Continue along the bottom of this beautiful valley. The path will veer away from the stone wall, where the area opens out a little.

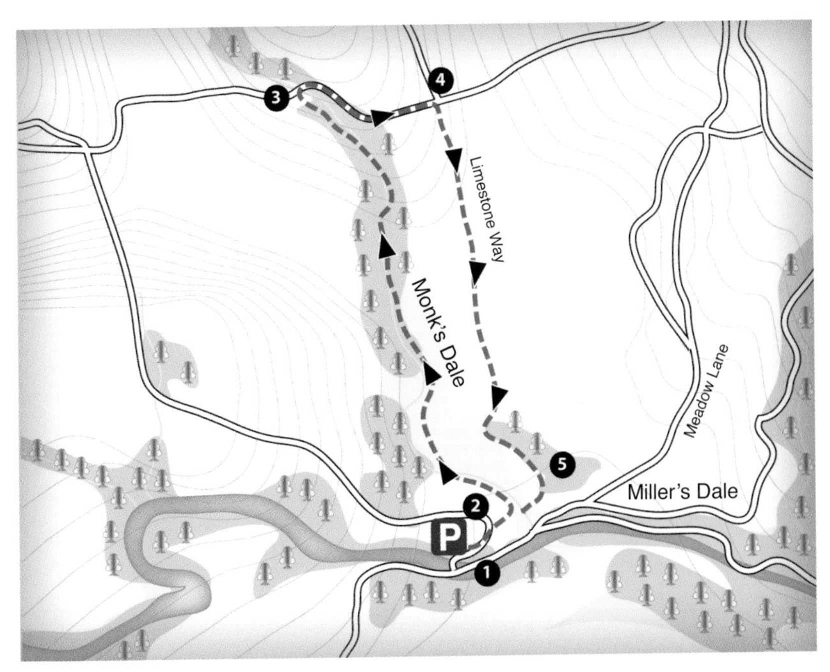

After crossing some exposed rock you will meet the stone wall again on the left. When you reach a path on the left, take it, which brings you to the river bed. There are stunning ash-dominated woodlands with ferns and mossy boulders. Walking in the bottom of the valley, there is a fantastic atmosphere with an ancient feel to the woodland.

Pass through a squeeze-gap in the stone wall and continue along the valley floor. The path is rocky, undulating in places, and stays in the valley bottom for some time. You will pass scree slopes on your right, at a clearing in the woodland.

Continue on and you will reach a gate in the stone wall. Once through the gate, follow the worn path across the meadow, with sloped sides. There may be cattle here. You will meet with a stone wall, with a squeeze-gap. This is quite narrow; therefore larger breeds of dog may not fit through. If not then simply turn around and retrace your steps, making the walk a linear one. Don't worry – you've already done the best part of the walk! Otherwise, pass through the gap and continue.

On reaching the quiet road turn right. ❸ Ascend, taking care as there are no pavements. Just before reaching the house on the left, take the bridle path on the right, signed Limestone Way ❹

Continue between the stone walls, with farmland on either side. Ignore a couple of footpaths on the left and continue until you reach the end. Turn right passing through a farm gate, again continuing between the stone walls.

The path is tree lined in places. Pass through a gate and continue between farmland, between the stone walls. You will pass a footpath on the right and then continue straight ahead. There are lovely views across the dale. Take the sharp left turn, with the wooded hillside on your left. Pass a house on your right and continue through a couple of gates, passing across the driveway, and turn right following the Limestone Way. At the bend in the road take the path on your right. Pass through a gate and then take the footpath on your right. ❺

Descend the steep rocky steps and follow the worn path, cutting across the wooded slope. Turn left, passing stepping stones across the river bed. Ascend once more, turning left when you reach another path. On meeting a stone wall on your left, turn right and follow the worn path with the stone wall on your left.

Now on a familiar ascending path, pass through the kissing gate, continue through a stone stile and turn left onto the road. On reaching the house aptly named 'Wrinkley Tin' turn right into the car park.

8. Miller's Dale

Medium - 4 miles - 2hrs

An amazing walk in the beautiful Wye Valley. You will follow the River Wye for much of it, crossing stepping stones and bridges as the river meanders along the valley floor. The woodland on the walk is beautiful, with fantastic rock faces and many spring and summer flowers. You will walk part of the Monsal Trail, a long distance footpath which is also a disused railway, and you will pass through a couple of railway tunnels. The Monsal Trail is also popular with cyclists. There is plenty of water for your dog. There are some high steps over bedrock, so if you have an old dog that struggles with his back legs it may be a bit tricky for a short section. After heavy rainfall the paths may flood, and in wet weather the worn polished limestone can be slippery.

How to get there – From Buxton follow the A6 towards Bakewell. Take the B6049 on your left signed for Tideswell. Miller's Dale car park will be signposted just beyond Miller's Dale village on the right hand side of the road.

Grid Reference – SK 138732
Nearest Post Code – SK17 8SN

Parking – Pay and Display

Facilities – There are toilets in the car park and a mobile snack bar

You will need – Leads, dog bags and sensible footwear

The Walk

1 Start this walk from the far end of the car park, furthest from the road. Follow the disused railway: it has exposed limestone rock faces, which were quarried out to make the railway. Keep your dog under close control as cyclists and horses share this path.

You will pass a limekiln on the right, and then before going over a viaduct over the valley and the river Wye, take a path on the right signed Chee Dale, descending the steps. **2** Turn right to meet with the river. Once on the path turn right to follow the river upstream. Dogs can cool off here as long as the river is calm. There are woods on both sides of the river.

The trees will clear, providing an open area with a stock fence on your right. Ignore a bridge on your left and a footpath on your right, continuing beside the river. There are rock faces on the left of the river and you will cross several boardwalks over areas that may get wet and boggy.

Pass over some exposed bedrock, with some high steps. There is lots of riverside vegetation in the summer, which can impede your view of the river. The path can get rough in places as you pass rocky areas. Pass over a sleeper bridge and then turn right. Just a few paces along ignore the path on the right and turn left, passing through a gap in the stone wall.

Cross another sleeper bridge, where you follow a stream that splits from the main river. The path begins to ascend and you will follow around a sharp right hand bend, meeting the main river again below on your left. There is another tricky rocky section, as you descend to meet with the river's edge once again.

You will now be walking between rock faces. In the summer months there is a mass of butterbur, a large plant with huge, round leaves and stalks which

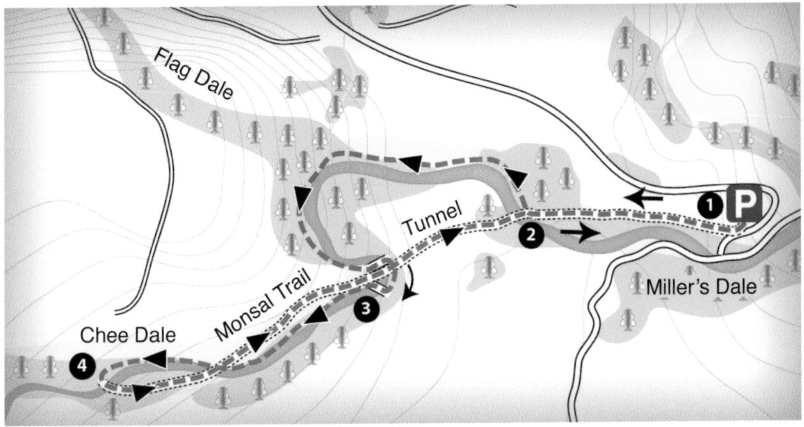

look like rhubarb. You will cross over tree roots and exposed bedrock and pass rock faces with mature ash trees. Cross another couple of boardwalks then ascend some rock steps as the path again goes higher than the river. You will pass alongside a large rock crag, which is popular for rock climbers.

On reaching back to the river's edge you will cross the river over large stone slabs, beside the awesome rock face. ❸ Then you will cross a wooden bridge over the river and pass under an arched bridge. Continue a little further, ascending once again, and then ignore a footpath on the left and continue to follow above the river. The path will soon descend, crossing another footbridge. You will have rock faces on your right once again and the river on your left.

Cross another set of stone slabs along the side of the river, passing the rock face on your right. Continue along this path for some time. The path will become narrow in places. You will pass a retainer wall, and then on reaching another arched bridge, take the steps on the right.

❹ Once at the top turn left, signed for Bakewell. You are now back on the disused railway line. Pass through the Rusher Cutting tunnel and then a little further along pass through the Chee Tor tunnels. Keep dogs on a lead whilst passing through the tunnels and be aware on passing through the first Chee Tor tunnel. There is a low wall, which has a big drop on the other side, so take care that your dog doesn't jump over the wall!

There are lovely flowers and ferns in spring and summer to the edge of the path. The last tunnel is the longest and has lights inside. A little further along you will cross a viaduct and then reach a familiar path. Retrace your steps back to the car park.

9. Goyt Valley

Medium - 3.7 miles - 2hrs

This is a wonderful walk, starting in beautiful broadleaved woodland with glades and meadows. Then you will follow a tree-lined river along the edge of pasture at the bottom of Goyt Valley. After an ascent you will pass a reservoir with lovely views along the valley. Another ascent brings you through farmland and onto the Midshires Way long distance path, with stunning views across to the other side of the valley and surrounding hills and countryside. There are cattle grazing for much of the walk, with some horses and possibly sheep.

How to get there – From Whaley Bridge take the A5004 signed for Buxton. Almost immediately after leaving the residential area look for a lay-by on your right hand side, which is not indicated from the road.

Grid reference – SK 008799

Parking – Free in the lay-by

Facilities – There are no facilities

You will need – Dog leads, dog bags

The Walk

❶ Take the footpath from the middle of the lay by and descend on the steep track, with a stone wall on your left and a stock fence on your right, with farmland on both sides. You will reach footpaths on your left and right. Take the footpath on your left, passing through the gate, keeping your dog under close control or on a lead as there may be sheep grazing.

The path is level now with mixed broadleaved woodland and a meadow below on your right. Continue following the undulating path as it winds through the woodland, with grassy glades. You will soon meet a river briefly on your right, where your dog can cool off.

You will pass a finger-post; keep going straight ahead, following the sign for Fernilee. Pass through a gate, and follow the worn path straight on at the edge of a field. There may be horses, cattle or sheep grazing here.

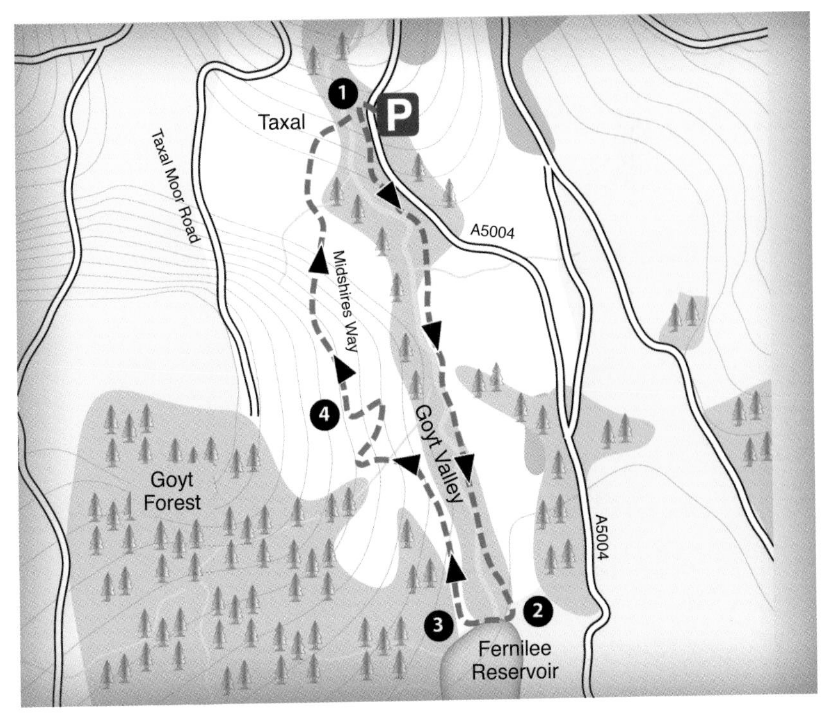

Cross the field and pass through another gate, then descend the stony steps. You will now follow the river at the edge of the field. There are trees lining the river and parkland trees across the pasture land.

Pass through another gate, still following beside the field, where stock may be grazing. Cross a footbridge over a stream. You will reach another finger-post. Ignore the footpath on the left for Fernilee and continue straight ahead. Ignore the path which crosses the footbridge on your right, and continue.

Pass through the small gate next to the river and continue straight ahead. The path will join a stoned track where you continue straight on. After passing through another gate, you will pass a substation on your left. The path is well made here, and you will meet an access road ahead. Keep your dog close by or on a lead. Pass a building on your left on meeting the road. Ahead you will see a Georgian-style building; turn left here and follow the access road, ascending quite steeply.

Pass a vehicle barrier on reaching the top of the road and turn right. ❷ Turn right to cross the dam for the reservoir. As you continue you will have views on your left across the reservoir and into the valley. Pass the water tower and at the end of the dam turn right. ❸

The path begins with a holly hedge on your right and a grassy bank on your left with scrub and trees. Pass through a gate avoiding the cattle grid, keeping your dog under close control or on a lead as there may be stock grazing.

There are views across the valley, with sloping countryside and woodland. Continue on the stone track, with a stock fence on your left, following the edge of the field. Pass through a kissing gate, now between the stock fence and a stone wall.

Ignore a footpath on your left, and as the path bends to the left you will pass a house on your right. Ignore another footpath on your left and pass through a gate. There are views ahead and on your right of the sloping hills, with stone walls criss-crossing between woodland and standard trees.

Ignore another footpath on your left and descend on the track. You will pass some exposed rock on your left, and then pass through a gate into woodland. Cross a footbridge over the river and ascend on the path, with a stone wall on your right. Keep your dog under close control. As you ascend you will leave the woods and pass through farmland.

Go through the gate straight ahead and take the sealed access road on your left, going through the gateway and passing a farmyard on your right. The road ascends quite steeply, passing a copse of silver birch on your left and a mighty oak on your right. Ignore a footpath on your right as you turn around a sharp left bend.

❹ Just before you reach the farm buildings and a farm house turn right, passing the farm house on your left, and continue straight ahead on a track between the stone walls. You are now on a long distance path, 'The Midshires Way'. There are stunning views on your right across the valley and surrounding countryside.

Pass through a gate and continue to the left hand side of a field, where cattle graze. Follow the edge of the field for some way, descending gently. You will pass a house on your left, 'Green Oak', and soon you will reach a gate at the end of the field. Pass through the gate and ascend on the access road, passing small paddocks and then houses on your right.

Just before you pass a church take the track on your right, descending past the graveyard and church. On reaching the river turn left on a path and cross a footbridge over the river. Turn right and then almost immediately turn left and left again. Now you have reached a familiar path, which ascends steeply back to the car park. Remember to put your dog on a lead, as there is a busy road ahead.

10. Hoo Moor

Medium - 3 miles - 2hr

This is a wonderful circular walk, beginning beside the Fernilee Reservoir, with fantastic woodland and quiet forest tracks, and views over the reservoir and the surrounding countryside. There is water in many places along the way, for your dog to cool off. There is a short ascent on a quiet access road and there may be sheep grazing in parts.

How to get there – From Chapel en le Frith, take the A5004 passing through Whaley Bridge, heading towards Buxton. On seeing a sign on your right for Goyt Valley turn right. Continue on this single track road, ignoring lay-bys and a car park. Just after passing the dam wall and on reaching the end of the road, turn left and then turn immediately right into the car park.

Grid Reference – SK 013758
Nearest Postcode – SK17 6GJ

Parking – Free in the far car park, passing the reservoir dam

Facilities – There are toilets in a lay by opposite the marina, just before you reach the dam wall and the car park.

You will need – Dog lead, dog bags

The Walk

❶ From the car park, go onto the access road. At the junction ignore the road that crosses the dam beside the reservoir, but turn left onto a footpath signed Fernilee Reservoir, crossing a grassy bank. Follow the well-worn path, with views on your right over the reservoir.

Pass through a kissing gate, keeping your dog under close control or on a lead as there may be sheep grazing. Take the lower path, beside the beech trees on your right. Ignore a footpath on your right when you reach the end of the trees and continue straight ahead, crossing the field.

Bracken encroaches the path in the summer months. Pass through another kissing gate, with views across the valley, and then the path will descend into the trees. Pass between the bracken once again. Descend the steps and turn left on a wider footpath.

❷ The reservoir is below you and on your right. You will continue on the path, where the trees change from deciduous to larch in several places. Cross a footbridge over a stream, then pass between old stone gateposts. Several streams flow down the hillside, collecting in a pool, before going under the path where your dog will enjoy a cool off.

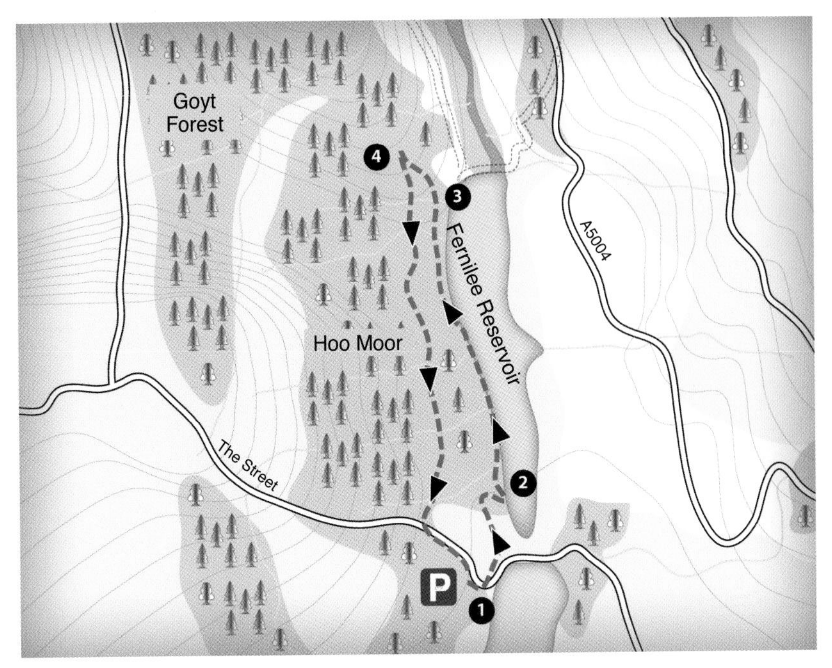

Cross a boardwalk over a stream. There is a series of steps as the path ascends, with a bend to the left, leading you away from the reservoir and deeper into the woodland. You will reach a finger-post on meeting another, wider path. Turn right here, following the sign for Fernilee.

Pass another pool on the left and follow beside the old stone wall on your left. Continue on this path for some distance, with several streams, where your dog can get a drink. Put your dog on a lead and pass through the kissing gate. ❸ Turn left on the quiet road, following the sign for Hoo Moor.

The road ascends for some distance, with views on your right into Goyt Valley and across to the hills above. Follow the switchback on the road, passing a double-gated driveway, and continue to ascend, passing through the pedestrian gate into Hoo Moor Forest. ❹

There are bilberry and heather banks on your right. Continue along the forest track, which is part of the Midshires Long Distance footpath. There are lovely views on your left, where the trees allow. Pass a track on your right and continue straight ahead. You will pass a block of silver birch trees on your right and then a boggy pond on your left.

Continue on this track for some distance, where there are some deciduous trees amongst the larch and pines. Look out ahead, where you will see double gates: your dog can get onto the road here, so keep him under close control or on a lead before reaching the gates. Pass through the small gate, cross the bank on the opposite side of the road and turn left.

Walk between the stone wall on your right and the road on your left, keeping your dog on a lead or under close control. Walk amongst the mature beech and sycamore trees, with views on your left. The path goes over old foundations of the stone wall a little further along. Continue on the bank, between the stone wall and the stock fence. You will reach a grass-crete road into the car park.

11. Lud's Church Chasm Chall. - 3 miles - 2hrs

This is a fantastic circular woodland walk, with a real gem; after a climb, it brings you to the most amazing chasm, known as Lud's Church. You will pass through the chasm and then onto an outcrop with wonderful views, following alongside a river named Black Brook, where your dog can get a cool-down. Sheep can get access into the woodland from the moorland above. There is only one, quiet road and you will pass through a small section of agricultural land. There is a squeeze gap therefore there is an alternative route for if your dog is larger than a Labrador, but there may be cattle on this alternative.

How to get there – From Buxton, take the A54 signed for Macclesfield, then turn off following the sign for Congleton, staying on the A54. Turn left immediately after the Rose and Crown pub, just before the hairpin bend, signed Quarnford and Youth Hostel. After going over a road bridge take the next right hand turn, which is quite a tight turn. Following the sign for the Youth Hostel, the car park will be on the left hand side of the road.

Grid Reference – SJ 998662
Nearest Postcode – SK17 0SU

Parking – Free in the car park

Facilities – There are no facilities

You will need – dog lead, dog bags

The Walk

❶ On leaving the car park, turn right onto the quiet road, which will ascend gradually. For dogs that are larger than a Labrador, follow option B. to avoid a squeeze gap.

❷ A. Turn right onto the driveway for the Youth Hostel. Keep your dog on a lead. Descend to the car park and turn right. With the front of the building on your right, turn left onto the footpath, following beside the hedgerow with a river on your right.

Ascend the path with some steps and pass through the gate. Continue on the surfaced path following alongside the stone wall on your right. Go through the stone squeeze gap on your right, and then turn left on a wider, worn path. There is a grass bank on your left and a hedgerow on your right. You will see a block of pine trees on your right.

On reaching a sharp bend to the left, take the path on your right, where both A. and B. re-join. ❸

B. Continue past the Youth Hostel and take the next right entering the Scout Camp. Follow the access track, passing a toilet block on your left and then turn right, following beside a stone wall on your left and passing a building on your right.

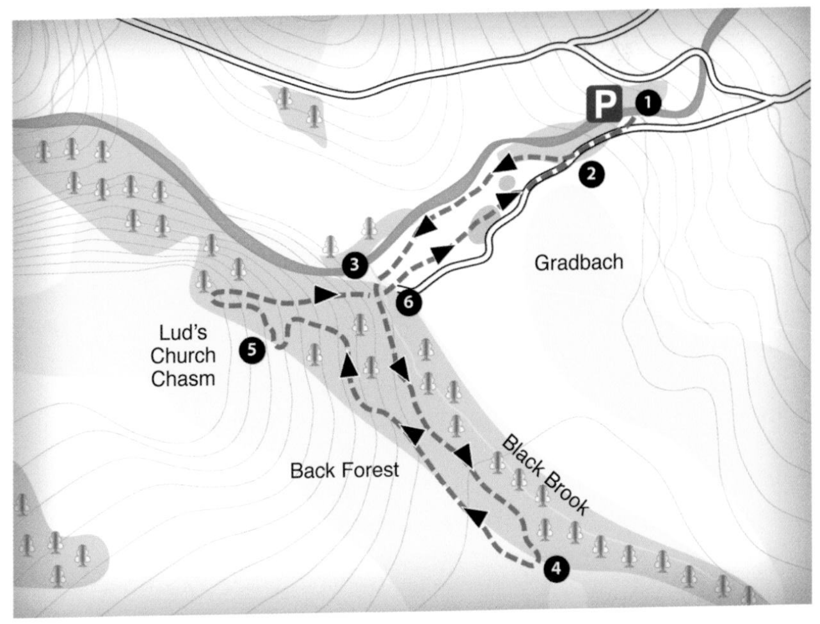

Turn left, passing through the gate into pasture land. There may be cattle grazing here. Continue on the well-worn path passing through a number of ungated fields. Then pass through a gate at the end of the field and follow the track. At the sharp bend to the right take the footpath straight ahead. This is where both A. and B. re-join. ❸

A.and B. Go through the gap in the stone wall, and then descend the steps. Turn right and descend amongst the wood pasture. Pass through a gate and cross the footbridge over the river.

Turn left on reaching a finger post, following the sign for Roaches. Continue through the beautiful wood pasture, following the worn path. On leaving the wood pasture, the path then cuts through the wooded hillside, with the river on your left.

Continue straight ahead, passing another finger post, where your dog can get easy access into the river. Continue through the oak-dominated woodland. The path ascends quite steeply at first. On reaching a fork, keep to the right and continue to ascend.

After the path levels out, pines and larch trees dominate the woodland. The river is now to your far left and below. Ignore the path on your left, and continue straight ahead, where the path begins to ascend once more.

❹ On reaching a finger post, turn right, following signs for Lud's Church and Swythamley. The path follows the foundations of an old stone wall. On nearing the woodland edge there is heathland on your left, just beyond the trees. Continue on the well-worn path, which descends for a short distance and goes back into thick woodland.

On reaching a finger post turn left, following the sign for Lud's Church and Ridge. Follow the worn path, ignoring a footpath on your left. The woodland is now dominated by silver birch. On reaching an opening, ignore a right turn and continue on the path straight ahead. Look to your right, where you will descend steps into the chasm, known as Lud's Church. ❺

This is a truly awe-inspiring place, as you will see when you pass between the rock faces, with ferns and mosses growing down the sides. Descend between the rock faces, turning left when leaving the chasm and continue through the woods on the well-worn path.

The ground cover is thick with bilberry, adding texture and depth. On reaching an opening in the woodland, you will see a finger post; turn right following signs for Gradbach. There are rocks in the opening on your left; if you take a detour to them, you will have views across the hilly countryside.

Continue on the footpath for Gradbach descending through the woods. On reaching a finger post, turn left to descend on the path following the sign for Gradbach. Ignore a path to Dane Bridge and continue straight ahead, heading toward the river. You are now on a familiar path; cross the footbridge and pass through the gate once again.

Turn left on reaching the steps to pass through the gap in the stone wall. Now retrace your steps back the way you came. For larger dogs follow B. once again.

A.Turn left on the track and continue to the end, where you reach the squeeze gap. Go through the squeeze gap and turn left. Continue on the path, passing through the gate. Ensure that your dog is on a lead and descend the steps and follow the path. On reaching the building, turn right and then left and follow the access track back to the road. Turn left on reaching the road, to descend back to the car park.

❻ B. Continue straight ahead, following the track. Put your dog on a lead or under close control before passing through the gate, and cross the farmland, following the worn path. Go through the gate and turn right, then turn left passing the toilet block. Continue straight ahead, turn left on reaching the road, and follow the road back to the car park.

12. The Roaches

Medium - 3 miles - 2hrs

This is a fabulous walk, with a linear section to it, following the tops of the famous cliff faces known as 'The Roaches". After only a gradual ascent, you will reach the most amazing views, stretching for miles across heathland, rolling hills and beautiful countryside. The rock formations, which are very typical of the Peak District, are fabulous. No rock can ever look the same, because they have been sculpted over millions of years by the wind. The heathland is at its best in August and September, when the flowers are blooming. Dogs must stay on the paths during the nesting period and there may be cattle and sheep grazing. There are several streams on the way to the top and a large pool where your dog can cool off.

How to get there – From Buxton, take the A53, signed for Leek. After quite a distance there will be two right hand turns for Upper Hulme: take the second one and then turn left. Pass the Roaches Tea Room and continue to the last parking bay, before you reach the house on the right.

Grid Reference – SK 000625
Nearest Postcode – ST13 8TY

Parking – Free in the parking bay

Facilities – There is a tea room before reaching the car park

You will need – Dog lead, dog bags

The Walk

❶ If you are ascending the road take the footpath on your right at the beginning of the last parking bay, signed Roaches Gate. Pass through the gate and ascend the path, with instant views on your right across the countryside and a lake and on your left to the rock faces.

Pass a path on your left and continue on a gradual ascent. The area is dominated by bracken, with some heather pockets. Ignore another path on your left that heads towards a building and continue.

You will pass an old stone post, then ignore another path on your left and continue. Ignore a gated footpath on your right, and take the footpath on the left opposite. ❷ Ascend toward the rock faces. Ignore a grassy path on the left and continue on the path, which veers to the right, with the rock faces on your left and panoramic views on your right, crossing over bedrock in places.

Cross over several streams, where your dog can get water. Keep the rock

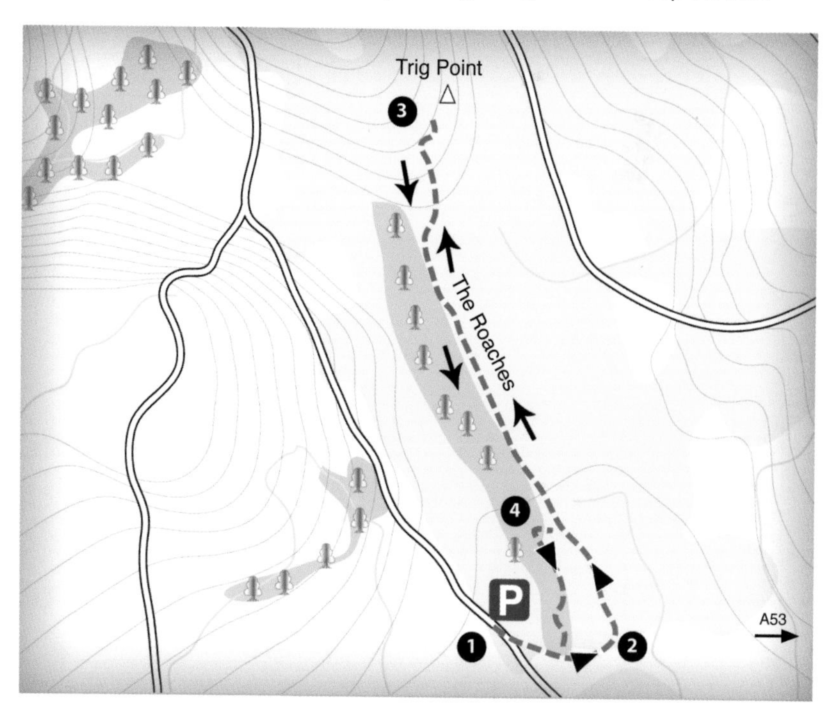

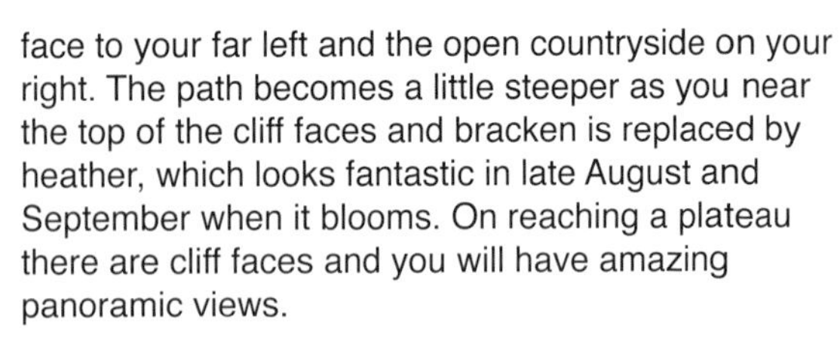

face to your far left and the open countryside on your right. The path becomes a little steeper as you near the top of the cliff faces and bracken is replaced by heather, which looks fantastic in late August and September when it blooms. On reaching a plateau there are cliff faces and you will have amazing panoramic views.

You will reach a dilapidated stone wall on your left: continue, where you will have another short ascent. The path now follows the tops of the cliff edges, known as 'The Roaches'.

You will pass a large water body on your right known as Doxey Pool, where dogs can cool off on hot days. The path is undulating and goes over exposed rock in places. The views are breath-taking, stretching for miles across hills and countryside in all directions.

You will pass between old stone gateposts, and pine and larch tree tops reach the edge of the rock face. The walk takes you as far as the trig point in the distance. This section is linear so you can turn around whenever you choose.

❸ On reaching the trig point (white concrete dome) you are now at the highest and furthest part of the walk. Simply retrace your steps until you reach back to the end of the dilapidated stone wall on your right.

At the end of the stone wall, take the footpath on your right, which descends between rock faces on a sunken path. When you reach the trees on your left, take the path on the left, passing between the widely spaced larch trees. ❹ The rock face and rock boulders are on your left and both are popular for rock

climbing. Continue on the level path, with sloping larch woodland on your right.

Descend on the path, passing a set of stone posts. Then take the path on the right, descending a flight of stone steps, which are quite steep, passing between the rock faces. On reaching a worn path, turn left. You are now below the cliff face. Descend another shorter section of steps and follow the path.

Turn right, just before reaching a gate to Rockhall Cottage, and follow the stone wall on your left. Pass through the gap in the stone wall and turn left. On reaching another gate on your left into Rockhall cottage, take the footpath on your right, just before you reach a stone building.

Descend the path and on reaching a familiar path, turn right and descend back to the road, where you have parked your car.

13. Lathkill Dale

Medium - 4.4 miles - 2hrs

This is a wonderful linear walk, passing under broadleaved woodland beside a beautiful, crystal clear river which has several weirs and a waterfall. You will pass an old mine shaft, the mouth of which is partly accessible. In the summer months you will see lots of wild flowers, butterflies, bees and wildfowl in the river and on the banks. You pass limestone outcrops and limestone grassland slopes. There may be sheep on a small section of the walk. There is one quiet road at the beginning and end and lots of water for your dog.

How to get there – From Bakewell take the B5055 signed for Monyash and Over Haddon. Take the left turn following the sign for Over Haddon and Lathkill Dale. On reaching Over Haddon village, follow the signs for Lathkill car park.

Grid Reference – SK 203664

Parking – Pay and Display

Facilities - Toilets in the car park

You will need – Dog lead, dog bags

The Walk

❶ From the car park, facing the toilet block near to the entrance, turn right and exit the car park via the pedestrian gate onto the road. Turn right and descend the road, which is steep and winding. You will pass a disabled parking bay on your right.

Just after the sharp bend you will pass a house on your left. ❷ Then take the path on your right, before the road passes between the house and the stone barn. Go through a farm gate (usually open) and then after passing the gable end of the barn, go through a smaller gate.

Continue on the stone path, beneath the trees. In spring and summer there are many wild flowers lining the path on both sides. You will pass a series of dead hedges on your left, which are used to prevent disturbance to wildlife. The trees thin out on the left and you will see a gully, where water was once diverted during the mine workings.

You will reach the river on your left, but sometimes it may be dry at this point. Pass between old stone gate posts, and continue on the well made path. You will pass some limestone rock outcrops on your right in places along the path.

A little further along the trees on the right clear, where there is a stock fence and sloped limestone grassland meadow. There are several very small caves in places, and limestone outcrops.

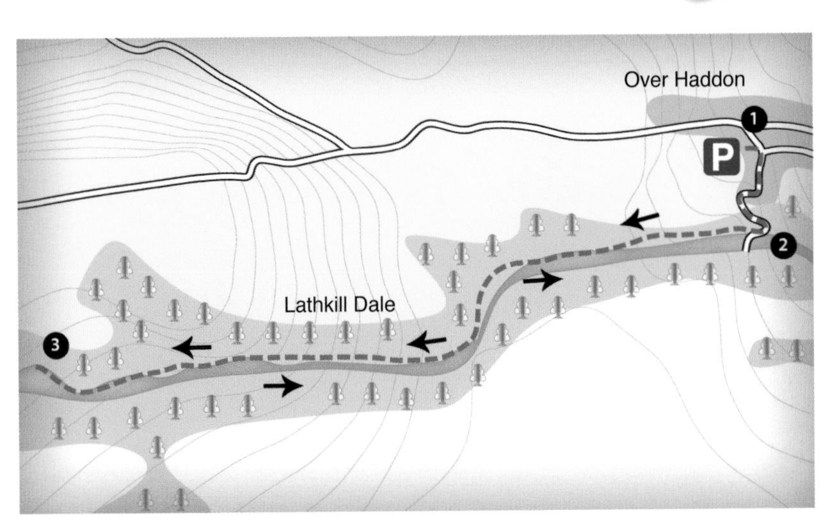

Natural England has signs along the river, asking people to refrain from encouraging dogs to go in the water. There are rare, white-clawed crayfish, which are vulnerable to disease. The water is crystal-clear and there are several weirs along the way. After passing between another pair of old stone gate posts you will have woodland again on both sides.

You will pass pillars, which are the remains of an old bridge. On sunny, summer days you will see many butterflies and bees, busy amongst the flowers, especially when walking past the open areas on your right.

You will pass a lovely wooden arched bridge on your left. It is worth crossing the river to have a look at the disused mine shaft. You can enter it if you dare, as long as you have someone to stay with your dog. Then go back across the bridge and turn left, to continue on your walk.

Further along the path you will pass a mine shaft on your left that has a dome grate on the top. The path gets a little rough with some larger stones. As you continue you will pass a couple of weirs and then you will reach a gate. Put your dog on a lead, or under close control, and then pass through the gate into a lovely meadow. Continue straight ahead and pass through another gate. Keeping your dog on a lead, pass through the woodland with a weir on your left, and just before going over a small rise you will see an old millstone on the ground on your right.

After a short rise the area opens up with limestone grassland on your right, but now there isn't any stock fence and sheep may be grazing in the area. You will then enter back into woodland, which is dominated by ash. A short ascent brings you to a small but beautiful waterfall. Stop here for a while and enjoy the scene. ❸ This is the furthest point of the walk; simply turn around when you are ready and retrace your steps.

14. Over Haddon

Medium - 1.8 miles - 1hr 30min

Very large breeds of dog will not be able to do this walk unfortunately, due to a narrow squeeze stile. If you are unsure you can drive to the Lathkill Hotel, where you can check the last and worst stile at the end of the road. It was accessible for French Bullmastiff/Dogue de Bordeaux, but only just!

This is a beautiful, peaceful walk, starting at the river, with crystal-clear water and several gentle weirs making a truly stunning scene. There are lots of wildfowl that also enjoy the water, with sections of broadleaved woodland and open areas of limestone grassland. Many wild flowers in the summer months attract lots of butterflies and bees. After a short climb, you will have stunning views across the valley. After crossing farmland you will then pass through Over Haddon village. There are sheep for sections of this walk and some quiet roads. There is water along the way for your dog.

How to get there – From Bakewell take the B5055 signed for Monyash and Over Haddon. Take the left turn following the sign for Over Haddon and Lathkill Dale. On reaching Over Haddon village follow the signs for Lathkill car park.

Grid Reference – SK 203664 **Nearest Postcode** – DE45 1JE

Parking – Pay and Display

Facilities - Toilets in the car park

You will need – Dog lead, dog bags

The Walk

1 From the car park, facing the toilet block near to the entrance turn right and exit the car park onto the road. Turn right and descend the road, which is steep and winding. Pass the disabled parking bay on your right and continue to descend on the quiet road. Ignore a footpath on your right and go between the house and the stone barn. Turn left immediately after passing the house to walk between the house and the river bed.

After passing the house and garden, you will reach a gate. **2** Go through the gate, keeping your dog on the path as you pass through the nature reserve. There is a wire fence on your right and woodland on your left. The path can be a little overgrown in places to begin with.

Cross over the exposed limestone. As you reach a squeeze post there are sheep on the other side, so keep your dog under close control or on a lead. Go through the gap and then through a gate. The scenery is wonderful here as you leave the woodland; there is a limestone grassland bank on your left, a fabulous river on your right and limestone rock on your far right. There is beautiful ash woodland on the other side of the river.

You will reach another gate, passing through into another area where sheep graze. There are scattered hawthorns and ash trees on the grassland slope. Continue along the stoned path beside the stock fence on your right.

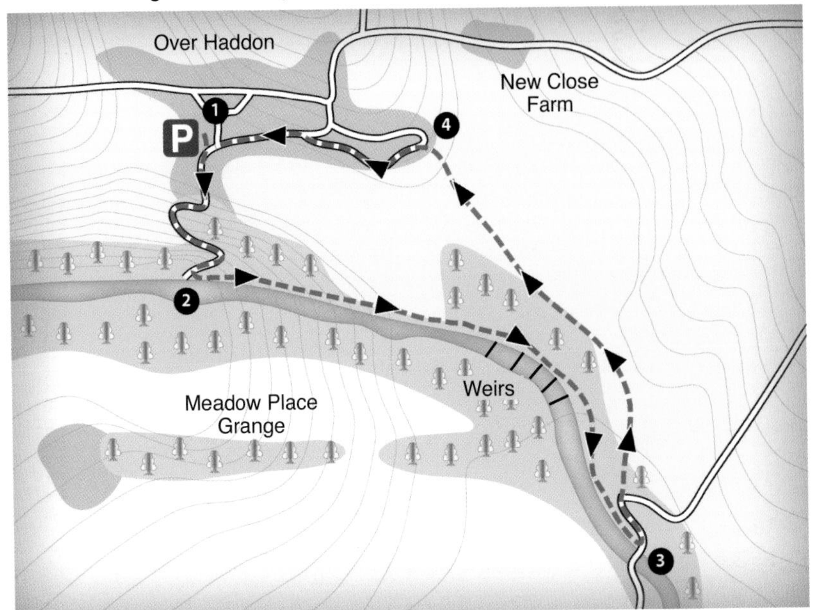

Your dog can get access to the water after passing the fence line at the end of the nature reserve. The water is crystal clear and has lots of plant life, with a series of weirs. Follow the river down along the path. There are many wild flowers in the summer months, which attract lots of butterflies and bees.

Look back as you go for a wonderful view of the river, as the water flows down the many weirs in the valley surrounded by trees. Pass through another kissing gate, now away from sheep, walking amongst the trees once more. As the path starts to ascend put your dog on a lead before reaching a gap onto the road.

❸ On reaching the road turn left and ascend quite steeply. At the sharp bend, where there is a parking bay, turn left onto a footpath passing through a squeeze post in the stone wall and ascend the exposed limestone. Put your dog on a lead or under close control and pass through another squeeze post, which is narrow so your dog may choose to jump over the low wall.

Turn left and continue on the edge of farmland, where a short ascent brings you wonderful views of the valley on your left and the river. Pass through another gate and continue, cutting across the middle of a sloped field. Now you will have clear views below of where you have walked along the river.

Follow the well-worn grassy path, passing several fields on your right. Pass through another gate on your right to continue with the footpath. Turn left and head for the stone wall ahead, veering slightly to the right. Pass through a gate and a gap in the stone wall and make your way across the field, heading towards the end of a stone wall, where the last house stands at the end of the road. On reaching the end of the stone wall pass through a gate and a very narrow squeeze post. ❹

Pass the Lathkill Hotel on your right and continue along the road. Follow the road on your left, ignoring a road on your right, and continue descending through the village. On reaching another road, turn left. Continue beside the houses and at the end of the road you will reach the car park.

15. Youlgreave

Medium - 1.5 miles - 1hr

This is a beautiful circular walk, and those dogs that like the water will love it. For most of the way, you will walk beside the River Bradford. There are many weirs along the way and woodlands on both sides of the river. After crossing a short open section, which may be grazed by livestock, you will pass through the quiet village back to your car. There may be livestock and there are quiet roads. Your dog will have plenty of opportunity to have a drink along the way.

How to get there – From Bakewell take the A6 heading towards Matlock. Turn right onto the B5056, following the signs for Ashbourne and Youlgreave. Ignore the turn-off for Ashbourne and continue. Drive through the village, where you will reach the car park on the right hand side.

Grid Reference – SK 205640
Nearest Postcode – DE45 1UW

Parking – Payment at the car park

Facilities – Toilets in the car park. Gardens have fresh produce for sale on last leg of walk. Village shop.

You will need – Dog lead, dog bags

The Walk

❶ From the village car park go back onto the road, cross over and turn right. On reaching a small green area, with a bench on your left, take the footpath ahead and to the left. Pass through the gate and descend the grassy bank.

You will enter into mixed broadleaved woodland and as you descend a little further, the path levels out and you will reach a river. Dogs will enjoy a paddle here, or a cool drink. Continue on the path beside the river. The path may get a little overgrown here in the summer months.

Pass through a kissing gate, on reaching a stone wall. Turn left on meeting another path, descending towards a stone bridge. Keep your dog under close control and cross the bridge, ensuring that he doesn't jump over the wall. ❷ Turn left following the river and pass through the weighted gate, on reaching a moss-covered wall.

The river has many different species of aquatic plants, giving colour and texture amongst the clear water. Continue on the surfaced path, with grassy banks, wild flowers and trees on your right and trees on the other side of the river.

There are several weirs made of stone walls and earth along the river, that slow the water down, creating a pond-like body of water on one side and a

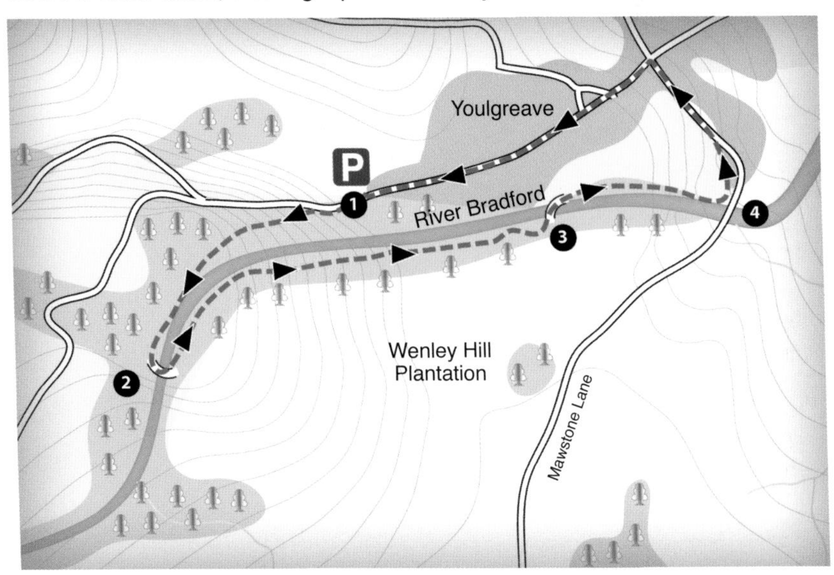

flowing river on the other. After a while you will reach a stock fence on your left, which prevents your dog from entering the water. When you reach a gate on your left, call your dog close and pass through the gate, then cross the footbridge. ❸

Turn right, put your dog on a lead or under close control and go through the gate, following the river again, with a grass hillside on your left. There may be livestock grazing here. There are lovely, mature parkland trees, with trees surrounding the area.

You will pass another weir, different from the others, with only a raised wall holding the water back. The water is beautifully clear here, with no vegetation so you can see the bottom of the river bed.

Continue along the path and on reaching the gate, put your dog on a lead, pass through and turn left on the quiet road, Stoneyside Road. ❹ This road ascends, passing cottages on the right, with cottage gardens on your left. Continue your ascent and on meeting another road, keep going straight on. Pass a church on your right and on meeting another road, turn left.

Continue along the road, through the village, passing 'The Fountain' on your right. It was built in 1829, when the area first got running water. Continue along the road, where you will reach the car park on your right.

16. Nine Ladies

Easy - 2 miles - 1hr

This is a fantastic circular walk, crossing beautiful heathland, with some silver birch woodland. You will reach a small stone circle, known as The Nine Ladies. There are views across stunning hilly countryside as you follow the well-made paths. There are no roads, but there may be livestock grazing throughout the walk.

How to get there – From Bakewell take the A6 heading towards Matlock. Turn right, following signs for Ashbourne and Youlgreave on the B5056. Turn left to continue on the B5056 following for Ashbourne. Take the first road on your left, signed for Stanton in Peak. After passing through the village continue on this road, where you will see a small interpretation panel for Stanton Moor on your left. Park on the roadside here. If you pass a sharp bend near a house on your left you have gone to far.

Grid Reference – SK 241628
Nearest Postcode – DE4 2LW (For Stanton in Peak Village)

Parking – Free at the roadside

Facilities – There are no facilities

You will need – Dog leads, dog bags

The Walk

❶ From the road side, go through the entrance into Stanton Moor and follow the path, which leads to a kissing gate. Go through the kissing gate and continue straight ahead, walking beside the stock fence on your right, passing under the mature oak and sweet chestnut trees.

There is a heathland bank on your left and you will reach a standing stone, known as Cork Stone. ❷ Take the path on your left at the stone and follow the path, passing a quarried area on your left and ignoring the path on your right. After a gradual rise there are lovely views on your left of the surrounding countryside. You pass a trig-point on your far right, then another quarried area on your left, which has a drop so keep your dog under close control.

Keep to the well-worn path, where you will have views on your right as you continue. A little further along you will reach silver birch woodland. The path will become a little unclear along the grassy glades within the woodland. Continue straight ahead, where you will see a fence line on your far left. Keep this fence line on your far left, and you will see the path once again a little further along. You will pass a small stone post on the path as you continue straight ahead.

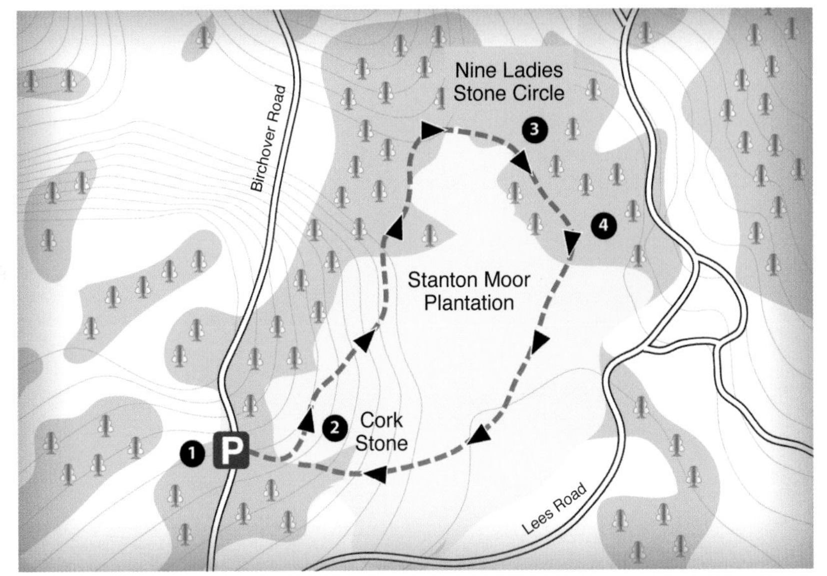

Continue along the path, where silver birch thins out to be replaced with heather and grassland once again. Pass a fenced enclosure at the corner and take the wider path, which veers to your right. ❸ The area opens out with a glade and a stone circle, known as The Nine Ladies. Silver birch trees now surround the meadow. Pass the stone circle and on reaching the obvious worn path, stand with your back to the interpretation panel and the stone circle and take the path straight ahead.

You will go back into woodland, where you will follow the wider path, descending through the bracken. You will reach a watchtower and a stile on your left. ❹ Don't go over the stile but continue on the path, veering to the right. On meeting another path turn left. You will have views on your left of the surrounding hills and countryside.

Continue on the well-worn path. You will reach a fork, where you should take the right hand path. You will see another stone on your far left as you ascend the gentle slope. Cross another path and continue straight ahead. Pass some mature oak trees and, continuing along the path, you will soon meet a familiar standing stone. Continue past the stone and retrace your steps back to your car.

17. Biggin/Wolfscote

Medium - 5.7 miles - 3hrs

This is a stunningly beautiful circular walk, passing through two impressively scenic dales – Biggin Dale and Wolfscote Dale. The walk crosses farmland, between stone walled tracks, descending into the dales, and then passes through a wooded section, surrounded by hills in all directions. Wolfscote Dale follows along the River Dove, which has several weirs where crystal clear water flows over, making it all the more pleasing. There is a squeeze stone that very large dogs may have trouble with. There are short sections of quiet road and sheep may be grazing in the dales. Your dog will find water along the way.

How to get there – Take the A515 from Buxton or Ashbourne. Turn onto the B5054 following signs for Hartington. From the village of Hartington, follow signs for the Youth Hostel on Hall Bank road and head towards the village of Heathcote. At the end of Hall Bank road, you will reach a grass verge/picnic area and Heathcote Mere. Park on the edge of this grass verge.

Grid Reference – SK 143601

Parking – Free at the side of the grass verge/picnic spot

Facilities – There are no facilities

You will need – Dog leads

The Walk

❶ Starting from the picnic site follow the sign towards Biggin, on the quiet country lane. You will have lovely countryside views in all directions. Turn right when you reach a track, ascending between the stone walls. The walls are low in places, so it is best to keep your dog under close control. Farm vehicles, cyclists and horses may also use this path.

Wild flowers grow on each side of the path in the summer months. At the end of the path, turn left onto a sealed path, then turn right onto a grassy track, again between stone walls. The stone walls are in good condition here, keeping your dog on the track. Gates into fields may be left open by the farmer when livestock are not present, so take care that your dog doesn't stray.

There are lovely views on your left into Biggin Dale and the hills and countryside ahead. You will pass a barn on the left. As you pass the remnants of an old stone building on your left, call your dog close or put him on a lead, as there is a road ahead. Just before reaching the road ahead, turn left and follow another track between the stone walls.

Pass a newly renovated barn on your left and go through the gate straight ahead, continuing between the stone walls. Pass through another couple of gates, continuing on the track. Keep your dog under close control or on a lead, before passing through another gate. You are now in open pasture land, where sheep may be grazing.

Descend the hill on the worn grassy path, passing between hills with exposed

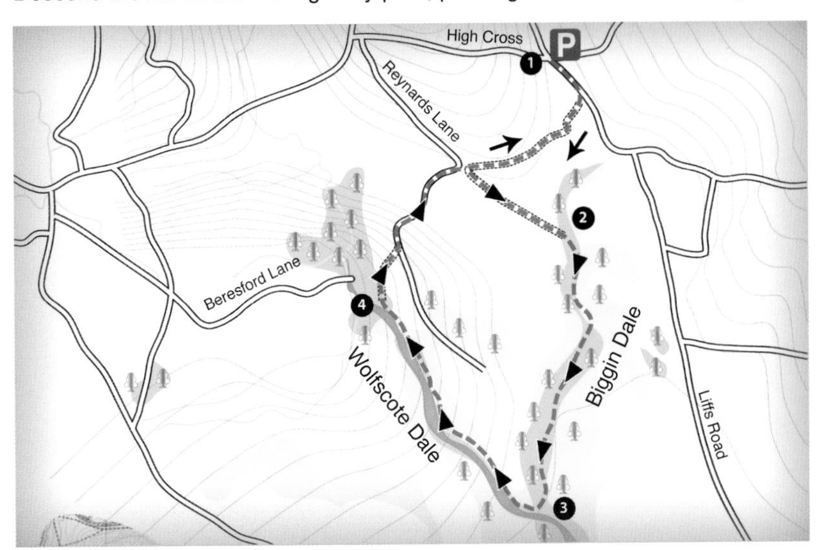

limestone. Follow the path as it bends sharply to the right, descending into Biggin Dale. ❷ Follow beside a dilapidated wall on your left. Pass over old foundations of a wall/building.

Take the path on your left, just before reaching the stone wall ahead. Keeping your dog on a lead or under close control, pass through a gate, where you will see an old mill pond on your right, then turn right and follow another path signed for Wolfscote Dale.

Continue following a stone wall on your right, surrounded by beautiful scenery. On passing through a gate the stone wall is now on your left. Continue on the path, between the hillsides, passing exposed rock and boulders, with ash, hazel and hawthorn woodland and limestone scree, all creating a fantastic atmosphere. Pass through another gate, where the path gets a little cumbersome with large stones, sustainably taken from the scree to the right of the path. The area opens up on leaving the woodland. Ignore a stile on your left, where there is a cave entrance. Pass exposed rock, with stunning views ahead of the hillside, mottled with limestone, known as Peasland Rocks.

You will reach a well-made limestone path; turn right here following the sign for Hartington, with the River Dove on your left. ❸ You are now in Wolfscote Dale. Once again you are amongst stunning scenery, with hills all around and exposed limestone. Your dog will love cooling off in the river, but check the water flow before allowing him in.

There are several weirs along the way, and the water is crystal clear, with alders growing along the banks. Continue along the path, where you will reach a gate, then pass through the squeeze gap, where the river has a stretch of private fishing. If there are people fishing, ensure that your dog doesn't enter the water. The path continues for some distance, and then you will see a large exposed rock face on your right, with a small cave. Soon after you will reach a gate. Go through the gate and squeeze gap and turn right, ascending on the track. ❹

Cross another path and continue straight ahead between the stone walls, with farmland on either side. Wild flowers grow on both sides of the path. Ignore a footpath when you reach a bend and continue between the stone walls, keeping your dog under close control or on a lead, as there is a road ahead. Pass through a gate on the top of the hill and turn left on the quiet road, which will ascend. Ignore several footpaths on your left and continue until you meet a sharp bend to the left. Take the footpath on the right and then almost immediately take the footpath on the left, signed Biggin and Heathcote.

You will now be walking on a familiar path. Turn left at the end of the path and then turn right onto a track, which will reach a road, so keep your dog under close control. On reaching the road, turn left and continue until you reach your car.

18. Thor's Cave

Medium - 2 miles - 1hr 30min

This is a short linear walk along part of the Manifold Way, which is a disused railway, walking beside the river for much of the way. There is quite an ascent through beautiful woodland to reach the impressive Thor's Cave, where you will have fantastic views of the surrounding countryside. The Manifold Way is also popular for cyclists, and can be busy on weekends and during school holidays. There may be sheep grazing for parts of the walk. Quiet roads.

How to get there – From Buxton follow on the A515 heading for Ashbourne. Turn right, following the sign for Hartington on the B5054. At the T-junction turn left on the B5053, signed for Cheadle. Turn left, signed for Butterton and Manifold Valley. At the end of the road, turn left into the village of Butterton. Continue through the village, following signs for Manifold Valley. After passing the church, take the next right turn, following signs for Manifold Valley and Wetton Mill. At the end of the road, turn left, where you will soon see a number of lay-bys.

Grid Reference – SK 094561
Nearest Postcode – DE6 2AG
Parking – Free in the lay-by
Facilities – There are no facilities
You will need – Dog lead, dog bags

The Walk

❶ From the car park turn left and head for the road. Pass the road bridge on your left and continue straight ahead on the quiet road.

Cross the road bridge over the river, where you will have views ahead of the limestone hills and woodlands. Pass a road on your right and then take the footpath on your right, ❷ crossing another bridge and then following the sealed path. This path is also popular with cyclists, and can be very busy during school holidays and weekends; it is better to keep your dog on a lead during these times. Horses may also use the path.

You will have farmland on both sides of the path with stock fence on your left and a stone wall on your right. A little further along you will have the river on your left, and you will see Thor's cave ahead in the hills. Take care if you have your dog off the lead after heavy or long periods of rainfall as the river may be swollen and fast-flowing. If this is the case it would be safer to keep your dog on a lead. Take the next path on your left, where you will be free from cyclists. Cross a footbridge and continue straight ahead. ❸

This is the start of your ascent, on a well-made path to begin with and some steps. The path will become rough in places. Pass through hazel-coppiced

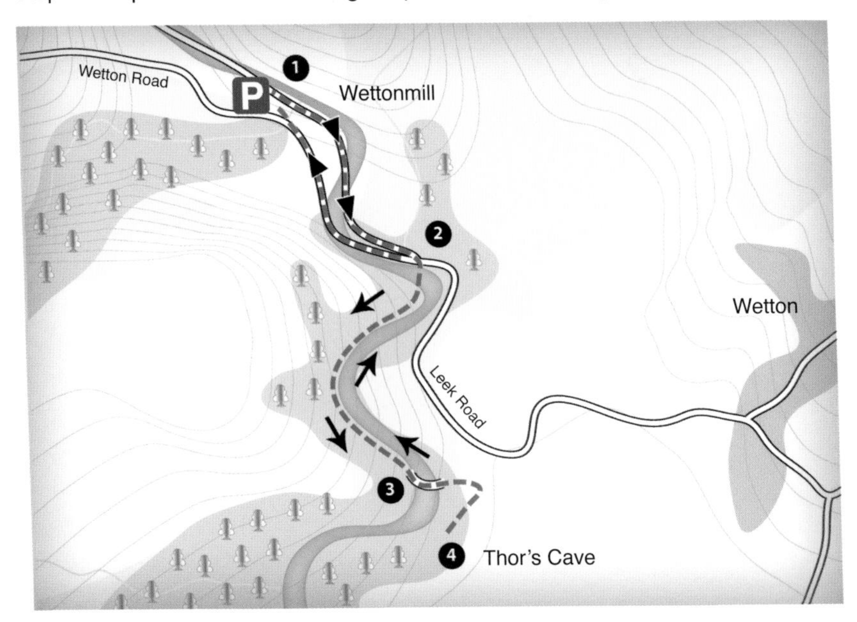

woodland, with ferns and seasonal wild flowers on the woodland floor. You will reach a finger-post; take the footpath on the right, signed to Thor's Cave.

On reaching a fork, take the path on the right and continue with your ascent. When you reach Thor's Cave the views are fabulous, looking across the valley to the surrounding hills and limestone outcrops. ❹

Once you have explored the cave (which can be slippery) continue back down the way you came. Turn right once you have crossed the bridge, back on the Manifold Way. There are more views on the way back, with mottled limestone hills and pockets of thick woodland. Remember to put your dog back on a lead before reaching the next bridge beside the road.

Turn left on reaching the road, and then take the road on the left, following the edge of the river. You will pass some limestone rock on the far side of the river. Cross a lovely old arched bridge and continue on the quiet road. A short ascent brings you past a stone barn on your right, and then the road descends.

Just before you reach the ford across the river, take the footpath on the left and cross the footbridge. Turn right onto the road and then turn left and left again, back to the car park.

CONVERSE
ALL STAR
POWER UP

19. Dove Dale

Easy - 2.4 miles - 1hr 30min

This is a linear walk, starting in the beautiful Milldale Village. You will walk along the popular route, which follows the River Dove, amongst stunning scenery. You will then pass through some wonderful woods, and beside caves and mature trees, with marvellous standing stones. In the open areas there are wonderful rock faces and lovely flowers during spring and summer. There may be sheep grazing in parts of the walk.

How to get there – Take the A515 from Ashbourne heading towards Buxton. Turn left on reaching the road sign for Milldale onto Green Lane. Turn left after crossing the road bridge and after passing through to the other end of Milldale Village, you will find the car park.

Grid reference – SK 136547

Parking – Free in the car park

Facilities – There are toilets and a shop in the village

You will need – Dog leads, dog bags

The Walk

❶ Standing at the entrance of the car park, facing the road with parking bays opposite, turn left and descend the quiet road into the village, passing the picturesque houses. Turn right at the sharp bend in the road, just before the river. Pass the toilet block on your right and continue straight ahead, crossing a lovely stone footbridge over the River Dove. ❷

There may be sheep grazing beyond the gate. Pass through the gate and continue on the well-made gravel path. Follow the river, with a grassy bank on your left and scattered trees. There are limestone outcrops on your left. In the summer months there are many wild flowers growing along the hillside and to the sides of the path.

As you reach close to the river, you will pass through a gate, beside a weir. You are now in a wooded section of the path. At the end of the woodland pass through another gate, back into an open area with a sloped grassy bank on your left. Trees line the river on both sides.

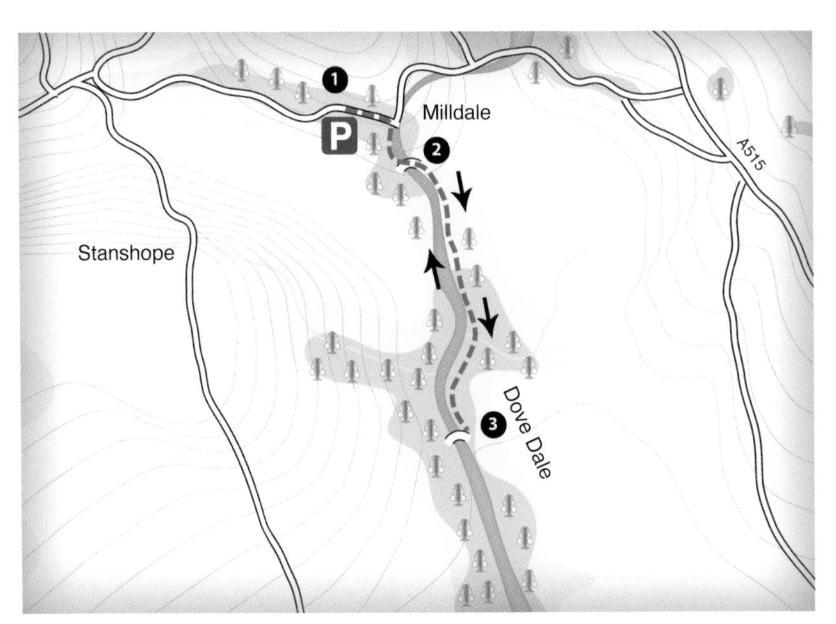

On both sides of the dale there are exposed limestone outcrops. As you continue, you will pass beneath the shade of the trees once again. Go through another gate and continue following the beautiful river. You will pass a footpath on your left, and then on reaching a limestone rock face on your left you will pass a couple of shallow caves.

The path will ascend for a short section and descend back onto a level path, with the river on your far right. You will pass through mixed deciduous woodland, with hazel coppice. A mass of meadowsweet fills the area between the path and the river in the summer months.

Pass through another gate. A little further along you will see amazing finger-like limestone outcrops ahead on your left and a footbridge on your right, where there is a large chunk of limestone outcrop. Do not cross the footbridge but continue to the limestone outcrop on your left, where you will see a small, shallow cave. ❸

You have reached the furthest point of your walk; simply turn around and retrace your steps

20. Illam

Easy - 3 miles - 1hr 30min

This is a stunning and very popular short walk in a beautiful dale, following beside the River Dove amongst fantastic, rolling limestone hills. A short section ascends a flight of steps to Lover's Leap. On your return journey, cross the stepping stones and walk back on the other side of the river. There are no roads but there may be livestock in the area.

How to get there – From Ashbourne take the A515 heading towards Buxton. Take a left turn following the sign for Thorpe, Dovedale and Ilam. On entering Staffordshire follow the sign for Dovedale car park.

Grid Reference – SK 146509
Nearest Postcode – DE6 2AY

Parking – Pay on entrance

Facilities – There are toilets and a mobile snack bar

You will need – Dog leads, dog bags

The Walk

❶ Starting with the car park entrance on your left, go past the end of the toilet block on your left and the mobile snack bar on your right. Continue on the path with the river on your right. Cross the footbridge over the river and then turn left. Thorpe Rock is on your right, and ahead the views are tremendous, with rolling limestone hills that almost meet at the bottom of the dale and the River Dove running in between.

Follow the river upstream, where on the far side mature trees line the foot of the limestone grassland slopes. The scenery is outstanding, with trees growing up the hillside and exposed limestone rock. The river is clear and your dog will love to cool off on hot days.

The path can be a little tricky if the river is swollen as you are forced onto the slope.

Pass stepping stones across the river and when you reach a gate, pass through the squeeze stones in the stone wall. Ash trees dominate the slope on your right, and alders line the river.

You will pass several weirs, which add to the beauty of the area. The grassy banks have many wild flowers in the summer.

Pass over exposed limestone, and then you will reach a stone wall on your left. Ascend the steps, where you will pass through woodland. The river is now below you. On reaching the top of the hill you will see a limestone outcrop on your left, which is known as Lover's Leap. ❷

This is the furthest point of the walk. Retrace your steps until you reach the stepping stones. ❸ Cross the river at this point and turn left. Continue on the well-made path, downstream of the river. Pass through the gate beside the cattle grid and take the path on the left, following the river back to the car park.

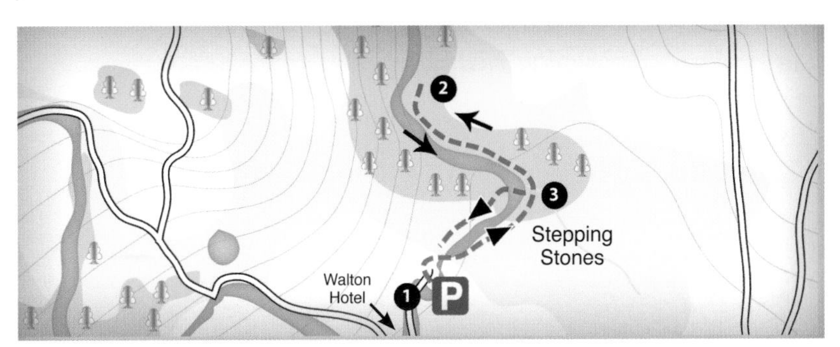

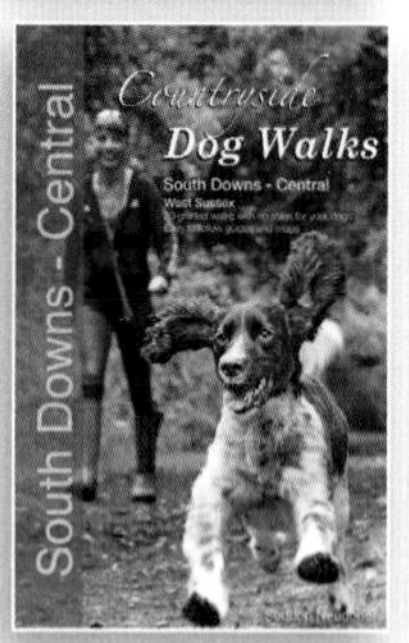

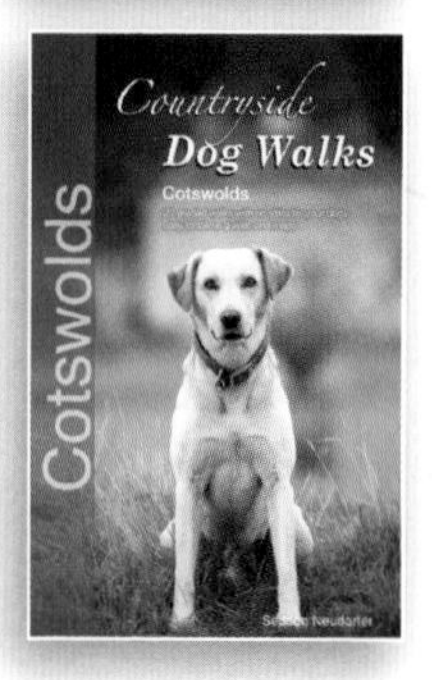

Follow us on Facebook for progress reports on our future publications.

Search - Countryside Dog Walks